Reconnecting the Local Church

Through Multilateral Ecumenical Unity

Having the glory of God: and her light was like unto a stone most precious, even like a jasper stone, clear as crystal; Revelations 21:11(KJV)

by

Dr. J. A. Gladney

Copyright © 2021 Dr. J. A. Gladney

All rights reserved. No part of this publication may be reproduced, distributed, or transmitted in any form or by any means, including photocopying, recording, or other electronic or mechanical methods, without the prior written permission of the publisher, except in the case of brief quotations embodied in critical reviews and certain other noncommercial uses permitted by copyright law.

ISBN-978-1-960853-00-4

Liberation's Publishing LLC
West Point - Mississippi

Acknowledgement

Much is owed to many people who have been an integral part of my life and development. Thanks to my wife Valeria Gladney for all of her support, time, and energy that she gives to our relationship and my development. Thanks to my son Joshua Gladney for his support of his dad. Gratitude to my late mother Magnolia Major Gladney and Father Henry Gladney Sr., mother-in-law Katie Suggs Moore, and father-in-law George Moore, and other family members. I also owe a great deal of appreciation to the members of Grace Paradise Fellowship Baptist Church and Red Oak Grove Missionary Baptist Church. I would not be at this point and have received my Doctor of Ministry without the assistance of Dr. Felix Burrows, and Dr. Kent Poindexter and my peer group (Congregational Development Church Administration in An Urban Setting) I am appreciative of the support that Dr. and Mrs. Lacy provided to me. Finally, I would like to thank God who called and enabled me to be a Christian striving to make a difference in the world.

Table of Content

Introduction 1

Chapter 1: Ministry Focus 5

Chapter 2: The State of Art in Ministry Project 21

Chapter 3: Theological Foundation of Unity 29

Chapter 4: Methodology 61

Chapter 5: Field Experience 63

Chapter 6: Reflection, Summary, and Conclusion 75

Grassroots Unifier 79

A Glimpse of Unity from God's Lips 81

Together We Can 89

Isn't That Good News 97

Building Up the Church 101

Biblical Leadership, Unity, and team Building 109

Now Is the Time for Unity 115

Questions for Sermons 123

Bibliography 145

Dr. J. A. Gladney

Introduction

Aesop, the famous writer of fables (620-560 B.C.) penned a narrative about a hungry lion and four oxen. The lion would often attempt to perpetrate an attack upon the oxen at the moment when they would congregate in the open field. However, the lion soon found that one lion proved no match for the united oxen. It happened that on a certain day the lion found each of the oxen standing separate from each other (due to quarrel that developed among the oxen). Now it became an easy matter for the lion to pick off the oxen one-by-one. Aesop's moral was that unity results in strength and division leads to failure.[1] (Redford, 2005-2006)

The truth in this adage holds true for all who chose to stand alone rather than together. In Griffin and Spalding County, the pastors and leaders in the Black church appear to have determined to follow the pattern of the quarreling oxen in the above-mentioned fable. Their apparent display of disunity contributes to communal disconnection, to the destruction of a unified witness of the Gospel and to a failure of the church in addressing the many social ills that exist in the community.

The writer believes that ecumenical unity can help bridge the gap that currently exists between the church and community. The current state of disconnection that presently exists can only lead to further division between the churches

---

[1] Douglas Redford, Standard Lesson Commentary (Cincinnati: Standard Publishing Company 2005-2006) 344.

in particular and the community in general.

Reggie McNeal, one of the writer's favorite authors, wrote a book entitled *The Present Future Six Tough Questions for the Church.* in this book, he intimated that the reason for one's failure to reach right results grows out of a failure to pose the right questions. (McNeal, 2009)[2] In this project, the writer focuses on the issue of ecumenical unity and wrestles with the possibility of creating a unified community. One the questions that is relevant for this discussion is, "Is unity possible?" in other words, can the church leaders put aside their differences and come together for a greater good that will affect the entire community? Another question that must be raised pertains to the issue of the disconnect that exists between the church and the community. Are there means by which these two entities can embrace their commonalities and use them to work together? This project seeks to provide responses to these questions and many more.

The information in Chapter One relates the writer's autobiographical vitae as it intersected with the writer's context in reaching the conclusion that a project on ecumenical unity was needed. This chapter also serves to explain in detail the rationale for the project title. A presentation focusing on the state of the art in the model of ministry is documented in Chapter Two. The importance of these models is explicated in this discussion. This chapter also deals with current and past literature that is relevant to the subject of unity.

In Chapter Three the writer lays out his theoretical

---

[2] Reggie McNeal, *Present Future Six Tough Questions for the Church.*

understanding of ecumenical unity. This presentation relies heavily on three distinct foundations: 1) a theological foundation of ecumenical unity; 2) a Biblical foundation of ecumenical unity; and 3) a historical understanding of ecumenical unity.

Chapter Four contains the methodology that the writer employed in the development and implementation of the project. The hypothesis and the qualitative/quantitative instruments used in the project are discussed in detail. It is in Chapter Five that one will find an implementation report on what was actually done in the project. A discussion on how the data was collected and analyzed will be found in this chapter.

Chapter Six provides a summary and conclusion section from the overall project. This chapter contains the writer's reflection on the field experience. Communities of faith have overlooked each other, walked around each other, and bypassed each other for indefinite periods. Prayerfully this project Will crystallize and focus attention on the need for ecumenical unity in the twenty-first century of the church.

Dr. J. A. Gladney

Chapter 1: Ministry Focus

Since slavery and reconstruction in America, the Black church has always been a natural extension of the Black family. Where else could a Black man who swept floors and held doors all week go to gain the humanly needed respect and esteem generated by serving as head of the deacon board? Where else could a woman called "Ole Sarah" all week long by white children whose very diaper she had washed, finally go at the end of the week to be addressed as "Sister Sarah Jones, president of the Missionary Society (Jackson, 1996)[3]?" The only place this could possibly occur was the Black church. Even though such scenarios could have happened many years ago, their vestiges are still alive. Grace Paradise Fellowship Baptist Church in Spalding County Georgia resonates with this rich history of empowerment for Black people in a time when there was universal denial of personhood for persons of color in the Diaspora known as the United States.

There is anecdotal evidence that shows that churches grow from divisions and splits. Many Baptist churches would not exist had a split from the mother church not occurred. The history of the Black churches in Griffin, Georgia demonstrates this evidence. From a group of slaves who were allowed to congregate for worship in the balcony of the white First Baptist Church of Griffin, the Mount Zion Baptist Church came into existence after the civil war ended. The

---

[3] Chris Jackson, *Straight Talk on Tough Topics* (Grand Rapids: Zondervan Publishing House, 1996), 88.

leaders of First Baptist Church permitted the ex-slaves to meet separately as a group in the basement of their church. from this group of basement worshipers that Mount Zion Baptist Church was formed. This august group chose Reverend Owens to serve as their first leader. (Faulkner, 1990)[4] The newly freed slaves constructed the first Black church edifice in 1867. This structure existed until 1909, when a larger building replaced it on the same site.[5]

Mount Zion Baptist Church, the first African American Church in Griffin, suffered a split in the congregation. The Eighth Street Baptist Church resulted from this split. Its initial formation began in the Spalding County Courthouse in 1893. This newly formed community of faith held her first service in the Excelsior Building, which served as a schoolhouse for Blacks on East Taylor Street. It is interesting to note that the Excelsior Building was situated adjacent to Mount Zion Baptist Church. After their split from Mount Zion Baptist Church, the Eighth Street Baptist Church shared the position of being the leading African American church in Griffin with her mother church.

Mount Zion Baptist Church served as the parent organization for another church, Rising Star Baptist Church, organized by the late Reverend Braxton in 1897, Rising Star Baptist Church continues as a worshiping community in Griffin, Georgia.

Grace Paradise Fellowship Baptist Church, the writer's context of ministry, developed as an outgrowth faith

---

[4] Richard D. Faulkner. Jr. *Griffin's 150 Years of Seasoning* (Griffin, Georgia: Faulkner Publishing, 1990), 65.

[5] Ibid

community from Antioch Baptist Church of Griffin. Dissatisfied with the administration of the church, several families from. Antioch Baptist Church departed and initiated Bible study in the home of Mrs. Mary Batts in 1994. They began to meet in storefronts until they moved to their present location at 1980 Futral Road. Reverend J. T. Harper occupied the position as pastor of Grace Paradise Fellowship Baptist Church.[6] In September 2002, Pastor Harper resigned, thus creating a pastoral void. The Lord led this writer, Jeffery Gladney, to assume the position of under-shepherd to Grace Paradise Fellowship Baptist Church in April 2003.

The Grace Paradise Church is located in a growing, yet rural setting on the outskirts of metropolitan Atlanta. Grace Paradise Fellowship Baptist Church is a unique church with a heart for mission. When Jeffery arrived at Grace, they were already doing evangelism and some outreach ministry. The Lord, through him, took it to another level. When Jeffery assumed leadership in Grace, there were only fifteen members. The majority of these persons were either related either through blood or through marriage. The membership has increased to over forty members since the arrival of Jeffery. The current population for Griffin, Georgia in the 30224-zip code (the zip code for Grace) is twenty-two-thousand-six-hundred-sixty-four persons (22, 664) according to Precept.[7] There are at this time in the United States over two hundred ninety-one million (291 million) people. In the new five years there is a projected 4.4% increase in the

---

[6] Ibid. 70.

[7] Precept

population for the area where Grace is located. There is also a projected 5.3% increase in the national population.[8] These numbers show that the growth pattern for this area is slower than the national average.

The rural setting serves as one contributing factor to slow growth in the area. The populace continues to migrate from the country to the city due to fewer job possibilities in Griffin. Therefore, ministry in this community must be exciting and able to hold the people's interests. In today's culture, music and relevancy are key elements to successful ministry. People want a God with whom they can identify. The church is called to engage in a transformative witness of God as the Creator to whom they can relate, and not just a God of wrath and damnation. The church must demonstrate that God is eternal and not just a Sunday-worship God.

Predominantly middleclass stratums of families reside in this area of Georgia. The non-Anglo population in this area is twenty-six per cent (26%)[9]. This equates to a mere six points less than the average of the overall population in the United States. It can be postulated that given these numbers, the voice of African Americans in Griffin is definitely silenced or muted. The voice of African Americans in Griffin needs to articulate in a more determined way if healthy change is to occur.

When change is needed, numbers are important. The writer has learned that the more numbers one produces, the greater the voice will become. Numbers also equal buying

---

[8] http://www.link2lead.com

[9] Ibid.

power and economic power displays a greater voice. Jeffery often wondered why issues pertaining to the Black community were often overlooked in Griffin and now he knows why.

It is of the uttermost importance that the smaller individual Black communities in this town unite in an ecumenical effort if their voices are to be heard, However, this requires deliberate and intentional efforts towards unification. Strength cannot come from two or three voices only. Strength emanates from the majority of the Black voices within this context.

The fastest growing segment of population in this area is the Hispanic and Latino community.[10] The overall population of the United States is experiencing the same type of growth from this segment of persons. The way the community functions will soon have to adjust to the growing needs of the Hispanic community. The average income for this population is $59,671, as compared to average income in the United States, which is about $63,207. The average percentage of single parent households for this area is thirty-three, as compared to thirty per cent for the whole of the United States.[11] These numbers point to the need for a community of faith that will minister to single parent homes.

This study also revealed that only 20% of the people in this area have graduated from college. That is 4% lower than national average, which is listed at 24%.[12] This information

---

[10] Ibid.

[11] Ibid.

[12] Ibid.

helps the church to know which groups we will need to develop programs to assist in this area so that God's Kingdom will be furthered. Too often the church fails to reach out and make inquiry from the community concerning the needs of the community. Instead, the church attempts to construct programs for the community without input from the affected community. Evidence of this can be seen in the social justice initiatives that the churches develop which are not accommodating the needs of the general populace.

Until the church starts to help meet the needs of the larger society, the church will continue to die and become a skeleton. The community where Grace is located resonates with the undertones of the Ezekiel experience. The query that was raised to the prophet Ezekiel asked, "Can these bones live again?" His reply was, "O Lord thou God, thou knowest." The Sovereign God is asking can the bones in this community somehow rise up out of the ashes and live.[13]

The percentage of current year population in Griffin encompasses the following: 73.8 per cent Anglo; 24 per cent African American; 1.2 per cent Hispanic/Latino; 8 percent Asian and 9 per cent Native American.[14] These numbers indicate that the Anglos maintain the greater voice. In an area that is rife with political undertones, effective ministry must take cognizance of the population of the area.

The buying power and the group with the greatest voice reside with the Anglos. There can be no equal opportunity in this area when the majority rules. In order for ministry to be

---

[13] Ezekiel 37:2

[14] http://www.link2lead.com

effective in this area it will have to be done with a political undertone or in a way that everyone feels a part of it. There are not a lot of multi-cultural events that take place in this area. Having such events may be a possibility for Grace to consider as this research becomes a living structure.

All of the above-mentioned groups are projected to experience substantial increase over the next five years as stated earlier. The Native Americans are projected to have the greatest number of people or the largest increase total. They are projected to increase by 14.2%. The Asian population is projected to have the next largest number of increases, 12%. Mother group that will change will be the Hispanic/ Latino population. This population will increase by 10.7%. The African American and Anglo population will not change that much. The African American population will only increase by 7.5%, and the Anglo population will only increase 3.1%.[15]

The faith facts for this area proved to be very interesting. According to an analysis of the faith traditions in this area, thirty per cent of the households in this area report no involvement with a community of faith."[16] Thirty-one percent of the households indicated moderate faith involvement.[17] These would be considered persons who attend church only on major holidays - Christmas, Mother's Day, and Easter. The number of households within this context that have strong faith involvement is thirty-six per cent.[18]

---

[15] Ibid.

[16] Ibid.

[17] Ibid.

[18] Ibid.

The challenge for Grace is how to minister to the sixty-four per cent of the people who have little to no involvement in the local church in this area? The harvest is ripe for the picking. The programs that Grace develops have to be community oriented. Of those persons in this context, eighty per cent prefer a historic Christian tradition. That is a very large number of people who want the old-time religion. In this context, only six per cent prefer a non-historic Christian tradition.

The remaining fourteen per cent confess to having no religious affiliation preference at all.[19] The overall faith receptivity level in this area is somewhat high. The people in this area will at least try to become religious if approached or if God through Grace intervenes. The overall church program category for this area is recreational as opposed to spiritual development, personal development, community, and social services. The people in this area do not display a marked desire for traditional or contemporary services.

The people in this study area have an average mindset when it comes to their financial support of the church. Their giving serves to indicate that they have met the bare minimum requirements for stewardship. The percentage of current year population by birth years for this area is as follows. Survivors comprise the largest group. Born between the years of 1961 and 1981. The survivors make up twenty-nine per cent of the study area. That is only .8% lower than the national average for Survivors ranks at 29.8%, only .8 per cent lower than the area under observation. The next highest group is the Millennial. Those in the Millennial group were

---

[19] Ibid.

born between the years of 1982 and 2001. This group makes up 28% of the study area. The most significant group in terms of numbers and comparison to the national averages is the Millennial. This group will range in age from 3-22 years old. Of course, the next largest group is the Boomers, who were born between 1943 and 1960. The Boomers make up 22% of the study area. These three groups make up the majority of the study area, which is 79%.[20] 18 Effective would need to target all of these groups.

These numbers will also help to explain the high incidences of stress in this area. Conditions which can contribute to placing an area at risk, particularly the children, are at an overall high level. This could be an area of focus for Grace Paradise in the future as God directs their plans.

The other two groups in this area are the Silents and the Builders. The Silents are those persons born between the years of 1925 and 1942. This group makes up 13% of the population area. The Builders are those persons born before 1925; they make up 4% of the study area.[21] The group that is projected to make the most gain over the new five years are the Survivors. This group is projected to make a 28% gain. That means those persons born between the years of 1961 and 1981 are projected to live longer and take better care of themselves.[22] That is very trendy today everyone is trying to eat right and stay healthy. So, the church would do well to reach out to this age group and get them interested in the

---

[20] Ibid.

[21] Ibid.

[22] Ibid.

church or reinstall church values within them because they are the ones who will be around the longest.

Grace Paradise Fellowship Baptist Church

As previously stated, Grace Paradise is a ten-year-old church that has had yet to develop its own spiritual and ecclesial identity. However, there are some unwritten rules that exist due to tradition. Some of these traditions have been easily assimilated and adopted from their former church. Nevertheless, with proper guidance those rules can balanced and shifted in the right direction for the church. Grace Paradise held bi-monthly worship services before Jeffery Gladney became pastor. They met on the first and third Sundays, with little or no emphasis being placed on the study and critical analysis of the Word.

This energetic group loves to sing and praise the Lord. The focus of the pastor/researcher became to recast the focus of the church from merely noisy praise to a mode of worship that combined dynamic praise and worship with prophetic preaching and teaching.

There were no active deacons when Jeffery arrived, which proved to be advantageous. Despite this lack in persons occupying leadership positions, the ministry realm has grown to include fifteen ministries and outreach programs that are focused on fostering ecumenism in the kingdom of God. Included among these ministries are Youth Sunday School, Bible Study, Watchmen on the Wall Prayer Group and Van Ministry.

Grace Paradise was already involved in the community before Jeffery began the pastoral ministry at the church. They conducted canned food and clothes drives for the needy. The church adopts a family every year for Thanksgiving and Christmas. When Jeffery arrived at Grace, he developed an infrastructure for the existing ministries. He clarified the meaning of ministry. Through his humility and obedience to the mandates of the Lord, the ministries of evangelism, community development, Christian education, and stewardship attained new levels in the church. Members visit and involve themselves with the homeless shelter and the girl's group home. The church has instituted a program called 'Take Back the Community'. Grace is also a site for the ITC off-campus classes where preachers can earn a certificate in Theology from an accredited university. Grace was and still is a family-oriented church.

The members of Grace are undergoing transformation. They were not accustomed to sound Biblical teaching and preaching. Due to their intransigence to the will of God being demonstrated in their worship life, their growth has been slowed. Grace Paradise Fellowship Baptist Church must shift from selfish worship to transformative worship if she is to be used as an instrument for ecumenical unity in the area. There are many concerns that these numbers and this report have shown the writer. For example, some concerns, which might exceed the national average, include school related issues, finding substantive spiritual teaching, access to quality healthcare, finding a compatible church, and teen/child problems. As an overall category, concerns related to personal/spiritual needs garnered the most attention abased upon the total number of households compared to the national average. The overall stress level is deemed to be high as a result of the at-risk single-parent households in the area. This is evidenced by noting that on the whole the area is somewhat above average in the characteristics known to contribute to community problems such as households below poverty lines, adults without a high school diploma, households with a single mother and unusually high concern about issues such as community problems, family problems, and or basic necessities such as food, housing, and job.

Based upon the assumption that as a group of people become older and more diverse, the potential for resistance to change becomes more significant. The area's potential resistance is likely to be somewhat high. What does this community desire from a church according to the research? In this area according to this study, church programs preferences, which are likely to exceed the national average, include divorce recovery programs, parent training programs, the provision of care for the terminally ill, active retirement programs and ecumenical unity. As an overall category, programs related to recreation are the most significant based upon total number of households compared to the national averages.

This community is full of potential and waiting for someone to offer Christ to it. Jeffery has discovered a lot about himself because of the process that this program requires; he has also discovered that he is not in the place of ministry at this appointed time by accident God directed his path long before he realized that he was doing the will of God or even in the will of God for that matter. The question that Dr. Felix Burrows continues to challenge Jeffery with is what did God send him to uncover within his context? Too often people run from the process before God has been able to use the process to effect transformation. These words clarify what is trying to be said, "Let God transform you into a new person by changing the way you think. Then you will know what God wants you to do." Romans 12:2, NLT[23]

The writer has discovered that his family infused two powerful assets into his soul: a deep-rooted and sincere passion for evangelism and desire to become an effective leader. Madame Eliza Jane Major, his grandmother, was a living servant - a great example of what he envisions the body of the church should be like today. She was a living evangelist. Yet she did not engage in claiming this for herself. She would help anyone at any time. On highway forty-five, where Jeffery used to live, strangers would frequently pass by walking. They would come to the house and ask for food and money. If Madame Eliza had money, she would give it to them freely. She would always leave instructions with Jeffery to this effect, 'Tittle Man, you stay with them until I return." Upon her return, she would dispense gifts of charity to the individual and the person would soon be on her or his way. Hers was a ministry that resembled that of the one God demonstrated in the life of the prophet Elijah. in like manner, Madam Eliza took that which others saw as unfit and leftover to nourish those in need.

Jeffery learned from these experiences and many others like that one from his grandmother that helping others is the greatest reward one could get in life. The beauty in it all is she was always willing to help those who she knew would never be able to pay her back in the long run. She taught Jeffery how to be a blessing to others. Her reply to him was, "Little black boy, you can be whatever you want to be."

---

[23] Romans 12:2 New Living Translation (NLT)

Because of many experiences like these, Jeffery developed and maintains a strong passion to help a dying world and care for those who cannot care for themselves. His life was shaped by his environment, his grandmother, and circumstances to help lead others. The Lord ordained him as a leader. No one had to tell him that he was a leader and not a follower. While growing up, he served as president of the youth department at church and became very involved in the community. Johnson Chapel Baptist Church was a part of several organizations in which he was involved. One was the National Baptist Convention of America. Dr. E. Edward Jones was the president at that time. The church was also a part of the Spring Hill District Association of Northeast Mississippi. Because the Lord had his hand on Jeffery and he had been trained for leadership, he became the president of the Spring Hill District Association Youth Convention. While in that position, he was called to several churches to speak on behalf of the convention and to serve as convention representative at meetings. The Spring Hill District thought enough of Jeffery to send him to Texas to represent the youth department.

When he graduated from high school, he went to Rust College and continued on the path the Lord had ordained for him. He became the chaplain for his freshman class and later in that year started to teach Sunday School for the All-Saints Student Movement.

While in college, he was also chosen by his peers to become the Superintendent of Sunday. He feels now that it was a job that the Lord had been preparing him for his whole life. However, the Lord was not through putting him to work on that campus. He was later elected to serve as the President of the All-Saints Student Movement, which held chapel service every day at 12:00 noon and conducted all the campus revivals and religious events. Because of that position, he was invited to cabinet meetings on campus and meetings with the president of the college in an effort to help affect change and foster a better campus environment for the students.

His leadership abilities came into play when he arrived on the campus of the Interdenominational Theological Center in Atlanta. Jeffery was instrumental in helping to organize one of the first Muslim-Christian Dialogues on the ITC campus. The members of the missions' department affirmed his leadership abilities when they elected him as the vice-president of the mission's society. Jeffery later became Chaplin of Morehouse School of Religion while at ITC. He also took part in a missions' trip to Jamaica. The trip to Jamaica taught him some very important lessons about missions and life itself. The same place where tourists see rest and recreation resonates with opportunities for empowerment of the indigenous persons.

The needs are great and the potential for ministry is enormous in Griffin and Spalding County. However, Jeffery feels the Lord is leading him to speak truth to power in the area of transformation of our spiritual community through reestablishing the Black voice in this context. The Black voice in this context is hushed, almost silent. At a time when a clear voice needs to raised, the community is divided, and the churches are experiencing dysfunction. The community is divided because the churches are divided and disconnected. The churches are divided because the pastors are divided. Jeffery often wondered why issues pertaining to the Black Community were often overlooked in this context, and now he knows why. It is of the uttermost importance that the Black communities in this town come together and make their voices be heard. But this will take a unified front. It cannot come from two or three voices only.it has to come from the majority of the Black voices through an ecumenical effort led by the local church.

One does not have a voice if the requisite numbers are non-existent. Numbers equal buying power and thus resulting in a greater voice the non-Anglo population in this area is 26%. That is only six points less than the average of what it is in the United States. This number shows that the African American voice is not strong because of the number of non-African American people living in this area. When change is needed, numbers are important. Jeffery believes that unity in this context established through the local church will help to seek the total welfare of this city. The job of the church, he learned, is not just to save souls, plant churches, or build buildings, but the job of the church is to seek the total welfare and well-being of the city. Therefore, this project, Reconnecting the Local Church and Community through Multilateral Ecumenical Unity, is of the utmost importance. This project will seek in all its efforts to build a multilateral ecumenical paradigm through the local church, which will in all its efforts seek to reestablish unity through the local church.

Chapter 2: The State of Art in Ministry Project

Several models of ecumenical movements or bodies could be focused on in an effort to discuss the state of the art in the area of unity. However, since this project maintains a focus on reconciling the disconnection that exists between the church and community, only those movements that directly relate to this area of unity will be discussed.

A model that the writer has found that closely does what this model is seeking to do is Racial Ethnic Multicultural Network (REM), a member network of the Association of Clinical Pastoral Education (ACPE). The mission of REM is to recruit, develop and empower racial, ethnic, and multicultural persons in their formation and competence in ministry and to enhance, encourage and enable the practice of ministry in institutions, churches and the community through education, consultation, fellowship, networking, and worship.

There can be no unity if most of these tactics are not utilized or engaged. The method from REM's mission articulates what this project is seeking to do across racial lines and denominational lines Multilateral ecumenical unity allows for discussion across denominational lines and racial lines as well. REM further believes the community's struggle to find a way to be faithful to different cultures and live out the knowledge that it is more alike than different are echoed in the fabric of society. If change is to happen, it will only come when the church takes the lead and embraces the responsibility for the people. REM also believes that church congregations and faith communities can truly experience an emotional healing through the integration of theological and psychological approaches.

Martin Luther King Jr. also focused a great deal on ecumenical unity. He was the leader of The Southern Christian Leadership Conference (SCLC), formerly known as the Southern. Negro Leaders Conference on Transportation and Nonviolent Integration. This civil rights organization was founded in January 1957.[24] The organization focused on non-violent civil disobedience and believed that it could use this methodology to gain the civil rights that African Americans lacked at the time. The SCLC was involved in many events during the Civil Rights Movement, including the Albany Movement between 1961 and 1962, the Birmingham, Alabama Campaign, and the March on Washington in the Summer of 1963.[25] SCLC is a now a nationwide organization made up of chapters and affiliates with programs that affect the lives of all Americans: north, south, east, and west. Its sphere of influence and interests has become international in scope because the human rights movement transcends national boundaries.

This project is seeking unity in the same manner as the SCLC and other organizations that came before it. The result of the type of unity that this project is seeking is unity that will enhance the education of our children, communities, and allow the African American voice in this context to be heard and taken seriously.

Several pieces of literature project clarity and understanding to this dialogue. There is no better place to

---

[24] Ibid.

[25] htpp://en.wikipedia.org/wiki/southern_Christian_Leadership_Conference,10-18-06

start a discussion about the literature concerning ecumenical unity than with *A History of the Ecumenical Movement Volume 3 1968-2000*. This great work is the third in a three-volume history of the ecumenical movement covering the period from 1517 through 2000. The World Council of Churches has taken the lead in selecting editors and writers for this series. The aim has been to provide a systematic survey of the churches quests for unity in faith and action during the nearly five centuries under review. This volume continues to follow the ecumenical story to the end of the 20th century, reviewing trends and supplying region-by-region accounts of developments in the lives of Christians. (Others, 1968-2000)[26]

However, there are noted divisions in our communities that are standing in the way of multilateral ecumenical unity. The division that has long divided our churches are discussed in great length in the book entitled *Ecumenical Pilgrims Profiles of Pioneers in Christian Reconciliation*, the fifty "ecumenical pilgrims" profiled in this book are among the many Christians of our century whose faith, prayer, work, and sacrifice have helped to break down the church's long heritage of division. The testimony of their lives is thus a contemporary challenge to new commitments to unity and renewal. In these brief portraits, the focus is not so much on biographical details as on the richness of the spiritual traditions, which meet in the ecumenical movement and enrich the life of the churches together. (Bria Ion, 1995)[27]

---

[26] Briggs John and others, eds, A History of the Ecumenical Movement Volume 3 1968-2000 WCC Publications Geneva, Geneva Switzerland, 2004 (4)

[27] Bria Ion and Heller Dagmar, *Ecumenical Pilgrims Profiles of Pioneers in*

There really cannot be a discussion about unity without the knowledge of Robert Brown McAfee, the author of the book entitled *The Ecumenical Revolution an Interpretation of the Catholic Protestant Dialogue*. This book is a definitive study of the ecumenical movement from its tentative beginnings decades ago to the present hopes for ultimate Christian unity. Most works on ecumenism have dealt either with the protestant search for unity or with the Vatican Council and Pope John XXIII. The Ecumenical Revolution tells both these stories, describing how new movements within both Protestantism and Catholicism have altered, the climate of contemporary Christianity. (Brown, 1967)[28]

Yves Congar is also a valuable scholar that helps add to the discussion of unity in his book entitled Dialogue Between Christians. This book has given the church not only the foundation but also the impetus as well to reflect on her pilgrim and ecumenical nature, the role of her laity, its priesthood and sanctification in the world. Father Congar here reflects on the Ecumenical Movement and its work, the encounter between Christians, and the schism of Israel in the perspective of Christian confessions. He ranges far and wide to present his thoughts on ecumenism in relation to Orthodoxy, Anglicanism, and Protestantism, and include his insights on the Christology of Luther and on Mary and the church in Protestantism in this great piece of work. (Congar,

---

Christian Reconciliation, WCC Publication Geneva, Geneva Switzerland, 1995, 19.

[28] Robert Brown, *The Ecumenical Revolution: An Interpretation of the Catholic Protestant Dialogue* (New York: Doubleday and Company, 1967) 35.

1964)[29]

There is also not necessarily new literature but literature that has been hidden from the public view because the author is maybe not a household name to those in the theological realm or circle, but to those who matriculated through the Interdenominational Theological Center (ITC) in Atlanta Georgia, they know this author well. He has written several books. His latest book that relates to unity is entitled Reclaiming Our *Roots an Inclusive introduction To Church History, From Martin Luther to Martin Luther King Jr.* This book is a collection of class lectures, notes, and a well of in-depth study by Dr. Mark Ellingsen, this book covers the eve of the Reformation to the developments of Christianity in the twentieth century. As in the first volume, Mark Ellingsen gives special attention to the history of Christianity in the Southern hemisphere, the church among minority cultures in North America, and the role of women in church history. (Mark, 1999)[30]

There are not many books that speak to an issue in such a way that once it is picked up, it is hard to put down and stop reading it or referring to it in some way. This book is one of such magnitude. It covers a long history of deep theological study that is second to none. The chapters include: The Ecumenicity in Perspective, Schism and the Ecumenical Ideal, The Ecumenical Movement, The World Council of

---

[29] Yves Congar, *Dialogue Between Christian* (Westminster, Maryland: The Newman Press, 1964), 115.

[30] Ellingsen Mark, *Reclaiming Our Roots an Inclusive Introduction to Church History, From Martin Luther to Martin Luther King Jr.* Trinity Press International, Harrisburg, Pennsylvania, 1999. p235

Churches and so on. (William, 1966)[31] The book is entitled Baptist and Christian Unity by William R Estep. This book helps add a depth of knowledge to the discussion of unity.

In addition, Alan F Gibson in his book entitled When Christians Disagree the Church and Its Unity isolates four key issues that have contributed to this fragmentation that this book addresses: Church Membership, denominations, doctrinal purity, and charismatic experiences. Gibson has brought together representative opinions from among divergent evangelicals. Despite any real disagreement within its pages, this book points the way towards the unity for which Christ prayed. (Gibson, 1992)[32]

As the search is made for more understanding and clarity about unity, the author discovered the book A *Guide to Christian Unity* by George L Hunt. This book was published in 1958 as an outgrowth of the North American Conference on Faith and Order held in September 1957, at Oberlin, Ohio on the theme "What is the Nature of the Unity We Seek?" which has now been revised because of the significant developments that have taken place in the search for unity between 1958 and 1963. This supplemental book takes into account the material written on these issues since 1957 and gives major attention to three highly significant developments in ecumenical thought since then. (Hunt, 1963) (Hunt, A Guide to Christian Unity, 1963)[33]

---

[31] Estep William R. *Baptist and Christian Unity,* Boardman Press, Nashville, Tennessee, 1966 (2)

[32] Alan F. Gibson, *When Christians Disagree the Church and Its Unity* (Leicsester, England: Inter-Faith Press, 1992) p 75.

[33] George L. Hunt, A Guide to Christian Unity (St. Louis: Bethany Press, 1963),

However, the book *Towards Visible Unity Commission on Faith and Order Lima 1982, Volume II Study Papers and Reports* is the best example of what happens when one brings great minds together. The topic of discussion is unity, but not only unity but how does one make that unity visible and able to be viewed as something for everyone. This book tackles that issue in a real way; it contains study papers and reports related to these two new programs of faith and order. (Kinnamon, 1982)[34]

The lack of visible unity is a problem in Griffin and Spading County when it comes to the Black church being out in the community together. It is that lack of unity that this project continues to come against.

---

[34] Michael Kinnamon, *Towards Visible Unity Commission on Faith and Order* (Lima: World Council of Churches, 1982), 144.

Dr. J. A. Gladney

Chapter 3: Theological Foundation of Unity

Michael Root says, "Ecumenical is a characteristic virtually all theology would claim for itself. Who today would want to be anti-ecumenical? Most often ecumenical theology refers to theology produced with the conscious intent of contributing to the recent movement toward a greater or more visible unity of the church." (Ford, 1997)[35]

Ecumenical theology is thus defined by a goal and a context. The goal is the visible unity of the church. The experience and perception have grown that the unity of the church is deeper and more resilient than its division. Catholics, Anglicans, Lutherans, Orthodox, and Baptist, all belong to the one church of Christ. That the churches nevertheless exist in division, refusing each other fellowship or communion in the Eucharist, has come to be seen as a contradiction of the church's true nature.[36] After all, Christ came "That all might be one."[37] Ignatius of Antioch says it was that lack of unity that made humanity so vulnerable to the forces of evil. Unity then was the supreme gift. It is through Jesus Christ that unity is obtained; it is only unity with and in him that produces true harmony among people. (Freedman, 1992)[38]

---

[35] David F. Ford, The Modern Theologians, (Malden Massachusetts: Blackwell Publishers 1997, 53.

[36] Ibid.

[37] John 17:21, King James Study Bible.

[38] David Noel Freedman, and other, eds, The Anchor Bible Dictionary Volume 6 Si-Z, (New York: Doubleday Publishing Group, Inc. 1992) m 752-753.

Therefore, the writer is of the strongest opinion that unity for a greater good is the way to help bring about harmony in this context. It is not about sacraments or rituals but helping neighbors in need. The Black community is suffering nationally and locally because of the lack of leadership in the Black community. Therefore, the church, which has always been the foundation of the Black community, is called upon to pull its resources together and speak as one voice with one purpose through an ecumenical effort.

In addition, the perception has grown that the division of the churches have impoverished their lives and their theologies, their understanding of themselves and of the Christian faith. Michael says, "An important force behind ecumenical theology has been the perception that in exploring together the shared foundations which make Christians one, we learn from each other and find new ways of expressing the fullness of Christian faith and life." (Ford, 1997)[39] At its best, ecumenical theology has sought not just unity but renewal in the foundations and fullness of unity. Why keep recreating the wheel? The wheel has already been developed and the model well tested. Churches need to help each other and stop hurting each other.

Michael does not think one can focus on individual theologians but substitute a communal or ecclesial mode of doing theology. His focus thus falls on the sorts of groups carrying out ecumenical theology and the kinds of texts they have produced. His argument is out of this survey some

---

[39] David F. Ford, The Modern Theologians, (Malden, Massachusetts: Blackwell Publishers, 1997), 538.

characteristics of ecumenical theology will emerge. His pattern of thought of doing theology breaks with the pattern of the virtuoso individual theologian. In his model of types of ecumenical texts there are several: texts from single churches, multilateral texts, and bilateral texts.

According to Michael Root, multilateral texts are produced by groups of churches gathered together in ecumenical organizations, such as the World Council of Churches (WCC) or National Council of Churches.[40] Thus, a study of these texts is required if one is to approach ecumenism in an effective manner. Out of the pages of history, God spoke to the writer and the theme that was to be undertaken in this context was slowly being birthed. The title, Reconnecting the Church and Community through Multilateral Ecumenical Unity, by reestablishing the Black voice within this context was slowly seeping to the forefront.

When more than one group is involved, it is railed multilateral. These gatherings are extremely varied, addressing virtually every sort of topic, theological, political, economic, and cultural.' Ignatius further says, "Thus unity is possible only within the church and is in fact promised by God." The ministry of Ignatius has been devoted to unity. As in Paul but developed even further, the Eucharist is the sacrament of unity. He goes on to state there is one flesh of Christ and one Eucharist. Therefore, the Church too, is to be one. (Freedman, The Anchor Bible Dictionary Volume 6 Si-Z, 1992)[41]

---

[40] Ibid.

[41] David Noel Freedman and others, eds., The Anchor Bible Dictionary Volume 6 Si-Z, (New York: Doubleday Publishing Group, Inc., 192), 752

Karl Barth was not directly or continuously involved in the business of ecumenism. Indirectly, however, his contribution has been fundamental to ecumenical theology. Adrian Geense says this about Barth's theology concerning ecumenism. "The scope of ecumenical theological reflection is to find and formulate a concept of unity of the church which might become operative for all churches involved. Barth's theology reminds the writer again and again that the source of unity, the reason for coming together is simply the common knowledge of and common witness to the love of God in Christ. The churches are invited to look away from themselves and from the historical conditions and obligations which prevent their unity towards him in whom they are all reconciled." (Bria Ion, 1995)[42]

Unlike Barth, Archbishop Athenagoras was deeply involved in the ecumenical movement. He lived out his life as one concerned for the rest of the world to join in a fight for unity. Athenagoras was convinced that the unity of the church and the unity of humankind are two closely linked ideas. He often remarked that Christian leaders ought to give up their defensiveness, come out of the trenches of the past and become fighters on the outposts of oikoumene, promoting love, Christian edification, and unity.[43]

One such stronghold of the Christian oikoumene, he believed was the World Council of Churches in which Orthodox and Protestants could cooperate as equal partners in a common effort to witness together to the world to help each

---

[42] Bria Ion and Heller Darmar, *Ecumenical Pilgrims Profiles of Pioneers in Christian Reconciliation,* (Geneva: WCC Publication, 1955), 16.

[43] Ibid.

other and to create conditions that would later lead the towards their unity. Karl Reiner suggests that the unity of the church is clearly an "essential" or "spiritual" reality based on the unity of God for empirically the churches are divided and disunited Kung and others have pointed out there really is no theological justification for the divisions in the church, which are the result of failure, guilt, and sin. (Peter C. Hodgson, 1982)[44] William Carey, one of the great forerunners of the ecumenical movement, agrees with Kung. Carey suggested that an international missionary conference be convened at Cape Town in 1810. Sadly enough, his cry went unheard for a hundred years later. Such a conference met in Edinburgh, Scotland. (Gonzalez, 1985)[45] There always has to be those who will sound the alarm for a change and that is what William Carey did. He started the vision even if he did not see it come to fruition.

The writer understands there are always going to be people who will say that they are doing fine just the way they are to keep down confusion. Consequently, Christians have stood idly by long enough while their communities have become filled with sin and violence. Division leads nowhere, no human in exile is free. Bernard Lambert makes a very good point concerning why the churches are divided. He says, "Has not the time arrived when Christians, conscious of the fact that what is lacking to Christ, to the Body of Christ, is also lacking to each of his member, ought to make their

---

[44] Peter C. Hodgson and Robert H. King, *Christian Theology: An Introduction to its Traditions and Task,* (Minneapolis: Fortress Press, 1982), 262.

[45] Justo L Gonzalez, *The Story of Christianity, Volume 2 The Reformation to the Present Day,* (New York: Harper San Francisco Publishers, 1985) 321.

voices heard above their divisions, and let it be known how grievously their separation affects them, that the absence of their fellows constitutes a running sore, and moved by a common desire for unity, look for means of healing, and allow love and faith to discover, to create ways that would lead each to the other?" What a confession of weakness to make no attempt! Many of the divisions among Christians which have come to be accepted as almost definitive prove to be only in fact a phenomenon of a certain period of Christian history?" (Lambert, 1967)[46] W. A. Visser't Hooft, a noted theologian, has attacked the divided church in this way. "What you have heard and what I have heard comes from one and the same God who speaks to us in one and the same man, Jesus Christ. We have one and the same hope of our calling- the hope for one and the same kingdom, If God's call to us is one call, that must mean that God sees us as one people, one family. We may draw as many dividing lines as we can, we may organize specific confessions and denominations, in God's sight there is just the one body of those who have heard his call and respond to it. God's Churches (sic) cannot be divided because its unity belongs to its very essence." (Hunt, A Guide to Christian Unity, 1963)[47]

What about this journey has hurt: the church? Evanston, in his report, once remarked that the unity sought does not require any group to give up its traditions, its loyalties, and habits. The principle of unity must be comprehensive. For it

---

[46] Bernard Lambert, *Ecumenism Theology and History*, (New York: Herder and Herder, 1967), 92.

[47] George L. Hunt, *A Guide to Christian Unity*, (St. Louis: The Bethany Press, 1963, 89.

is not until unity hurts-by requiring people to subject some treasured habit to a larger good, or to surrender some human practice to God's claim that they learn its real meaning or receive its deepest blessing.[48] The issue then becomes what is the church willing to give up for the greater good of all humankind in this context. The church must always be mindful of the fact that no sacrifice can be made that is greater than the cross of Christ. Oberlin helps Evanston to further this discussion. He said to proclaim that Christ is the one Lord is to give him pre-eminence over all else - even over one's most cherished traditions.[49]

Dietrich Bonhoffer would say the church is only giving God what is his. His key thesis was "The church is Christ 'existing in community.'" In all his subsequent writing, as in his tireless struggles for health and integrity of the Confessing Church, what rings out is this sense of the church as Christ's own body, Christ own hands and voice, and so not subjected to any conventional worldly expectations or patterns of humanity. (Bria Ion, 1995)[50] If the church is as Bonhoffer said, Christ existing in community, how is the church living out that reality in its various contexts? If the communities are divided, is Christ divided, or has the focus just become distorted?

John XXIII says these words quantity-sheer weight of numbers-is never in the long term more powerful than

---

[48] Ibid.

[49] Ibid.

[50] Bria Ion and Heller Darmar, *Ecumenical Pilgrims Profiles of Pioneers in Christian Reconciliation,* (Geneva: WCC Publication, 1995), 45.

quality, but if the quality itself deteriorates the greater is bound to submerge the lesser. In other words, the Church's struggle is a struggle for survival, and not only of the Roman Church but of ail Christian churches. The significance of the ecumenical movement is, in fact, no different from that of the Council (WCC): both are born of the same urgent need to seek safety. For this reason, they have come together, and the Christian world strives to present a united front against what has been defined in religio-racial terms as the new barbarian invasion." (Carlo, 1664)[51] D. T. Niles would say that John needs to define the barbarian and its function. The church is never separated from the task of unity or evangelism. D.T. Niles remembers a conversation he had with Dr. Kraemer in Ceylon. Dr. Kraemer's words when he left Ceylon were, "The Church in Ceylon is isolated and undistinguishable." How true! Niles goes on to further the thought. He is of the opinion that when Christians and non-Christians meet, the evangelistic encounter does not take place. They meet in the banks, they meet in the shop, they meet in the courthouse, and they meet in the hospital. Where Christians and non-Christians meet, the encounter does not take place. The Christian community is isolated, but it is also undistinguishable. They live the same kind of life as the others. The Christian community needs to be identified and distinguishable. (Jurjii, 1982)[52] What an awesome remark when bearing in mind the present context and unity along

---

[51] Falconi Carlo, Pope John and the Ecumenical Council, (New York: The World Publicizing Company, 1664), 42.

[52] Edward Jurjii, The Ecumenical Era in Church and Society, (New York: The Macmillan Company, 1982), 206-207

with the evangelistic efforts that have been made to set the church apart. The lack of unity can be a part of the visibility effort that Niles is expounding upon.

The question then becomes what has the church done to set itself apart from the secular world for the greater good of all people? What difference, if any, is the church making in this context. The disunification of the church does not help the visibility of the church at all.

Theoretical Foundation for Unity

The Black church has no challenger as the cultural womb of the Black community. Not only did it give birth to new institutions such as schools, banks, insurance companies, and low-income housing, but it also provided an academy and an arena for political activities, and it nurtured young talent for musical, dramatic, and artistic, development. E. Franklin Frazier's apt descriptive phrase, "nation within a nation," pointed to these multifarious levels of community involvement found in the black church. (Erica C. Lincoln, 1990)[53] This solid foundation that the Black community once stood on is divided. That division is creating barriers within this context.

How will a unified Griffin look? What will be accomplished because of this ecumenical movement started in Grace Paradise? How Will it impact this context and community? If this division is dealt with, what will Griffin look like? These questions are raised and wrestled with in an

---

[53] Erica C. Lincoln and Lawrence H. Mamiya, *The Black Church in the African American Experience*, (Raleigh: Duke University Press, 1990), 8.

attempt to help give direction to the discussion. To establish more of a backdrop for this discussion, the writer will begin by looking at what unity once looked like in this context The ministers' union and clergy association has long been dormant in this context. The ministers, who once lead the movement, lost interest and some have gone on to be with the Lord. Because Baptists are autonomous churches, the question is always united for what cause. Churches have their own programs that direct their attention. In January of 2005, for the first time in the history of Baptist conventions, all four of the major Baptist Convention's came together in Nashville, Tennessee. Dr. Gardner C. Taylor, Pastor Emeritus of Concord Missionary Baptist Church, Brooklyn, New York, was at the forefront of the movement to come together. At that time, Dr. E. Edwards Jones was still president of the National Baptist Convention of America, Inc. After much coordinating, meetings, teleconferencing, traveling, strategizing, and praying, it became reality the week of January 24-28, 2005, at the Gaylord Opryland Hotel, Nashville, Tennessee.[54]

There were a lot of positive things that came out of this united effort on the part of the national bodies. The most important accomplishment was that unity is possible even among bodies that have been steep in their tradition and way of doing things. The last act of business while in Nashville was the act of the Lord's supper. The conventions broke bread together and rejoiced in the Lord on that Holy Hill. At the age of seventy-seven, Gandhi undertook an exhausting tour from village to village in a country where murder, violence, and

---

[54] http://www.NBCA.com

vengeance were rife. He intentionally took care to lodge with the Mohammedans and search out their organizations. When he was asked why he took such pains and exposed himself to so much danger, he finally he replied, 'during my tour I wish to assure the villagers to the best of my capacity that I bear not the least towards any. I can prove this only by living and moving among those who mistrust me. (Cougar, 1964)[55]

Gandhi has shown the church ways to accomplish unity by becoming more visible through actions and deeds. There have been many causes that have cried out for attention, but the cries have only fallen on deaf ears because of the availability of someone to make a difference in those areas. What then is the task of the ecumenical movement? Its aim is to let the given unity become "visible." The predicate of visibility did not always appear as such in the description of the aim of ecumenicity, the unity of the church, and did not have the status that is accorded in recent times. But the idea if visibility was expressed alternately as follows: that the one life of the one body should be made manifest before the world, that the task was to give expression to the oneness of the church of Jesus Christ, to bring it into the light of day, truly to represent it, or to cause it to appear outwardly. (Meyer, 1999)[56]

On the eve of his Crucifixion, Jesus prayed that his followers "may all be one" (John 17:21). Christians believe

---

[55] Yves Cougar, Dialogue Between Christians, (Westminster, Maryland: The Newman Press, 1964), 56.

[56] Harding Meyer, That All May Be One Perceptions and Models of Ecumenicity, (Grand Rapids: William B. Eerdmans Publishing Company, 1999), 11.

that this promise is fulfilled in the church. The church is Christ's body, and his body cannot be divided or disconnected. Yet churches live in contradiction to that promise. The pursuit of unity will require more than a few mutual adjustments among the churches. Ecumenism must involve true conversion of both hearts and minds, of the will and the intellect. Grace Paradise must learn to think in new ways about the teachings and practices of the Church. Division has become deeply embedded in the everyday life and thought of the churches. Thinking beyond division will require a new outlook. (Ola Tjorhom, 2004)[57]

What a statement of weakness to do nothing at all if the church sees a need and does not address it. The oikos (household home) of faith in this context is depending on the solidarity of the churches to help make a change.

The structured visibility of church unity corresponds with the structured visibility of the church itself, in the sense that fellowship between visible church bodies must be visibly embodied, the church is a body and no mere idea or societas platonica, as a body it both has needs structures or as a reflex of the need for such structures. St. Paul's presentation of the church as Christ's body in I Corinthians 12 can implicitly be read as an account of ecclesial and ecumenical structures or as a reflex of the need for such structures.[58]

What that says to this context is this that unity cannot just be lip service; it has to be a lived reality. If one does not do it, he does not believe it. The church says it does a lot of things,

---

[57] Ola Tjorham, Visible Church-Visible Unity Ecumenical Ecclesiology and "The Great Tradition of the Church:

[58] Ibid.

but its actions are totally opposite. What is at stake is not some kind of obsession with structures per say. The key point is simply that a divided world - God's divided world - may see the Church and its unity and realize that the Church is a stage on the way toward the restoration of the world's own unity. This cannot be achieved through invisible fellowship, static diversity, or mere coexistence. The church can be a forceful and effective sign of unity in a world marked by militant division and massive discrimination only when its unity is concretely recognizable.[59]

Travis Smiley wrote That is *Black Love*. In the book, he vividly explained the power behind Black love. His description of Black love can be described as a type of unity within the Black community that is missing in today's context. Black love is powerful force. He says, "One of the challenges we face as Black people is whether or not we can take the notion of Black love and use it proactively, as opposed to reactively. The Black community has a way of coming together and rescuing each other and lifting each other up when someone has been attacked, undermined, or otherwise disenfranchised, but the challenge for African Americans is to act proactively with regard to the important issues in the community. (Smiley, 2002)[60]

To use what he has said as a unity concept helps strengthen this discussion. If the church and community come together, not just when a need is felt to come together, bonds will be stronger. The demonstration of love, not just Black

---

[59] Ibid.

[60] Travis Smiley, *Keeping the Faith*, (New York: Random House, Inc. 2002), 3.

love, will enforce the efforts of unity. In this pilgrimage, there is always for Christians a double command - to search for what God wants for his Church and to search for what he intends for the whole inhabited creation, the oikoumene. There is always a need to get churches to move from competition against each other and move to doing ministry with each other. Each church has to realize that the other church is in fact a church and that they are not the only ones who know God or can get a prayer through. Unity is collaboration at its best, which calls the community together in an agreement to work out large numbers of central concerns. The church has forgotten its missiological mandate. The church's main mission is to the world, that mission consists of bringing people to God's salvation in Christ. Goodwin put it this way. "Whatever its specific expression, a church is a church is a church. And if it is a church, it has one Lord; one faith; and despite the differences of interpretation, one authority in scripture, one expression in baptism and one fellowship in unity." (Goodwin, 1995)[61]

Biblical Meaning of Unity

The purpose of this section is to establish a Biblical foundation that will show evidence of a solid understanding of unity. According to dictionary.com, unity is defined as the following: unity is a noun, which means the condition of being one: oneness, singleness, singularity. It also means harmonious mutual understanding: accord, agreement,

---

[61] Everett Goodwin, The New Hiscox Guide for Baptist Churches, (Valley Forge, PA., Johnson Press, 1995), 212.

concord, concordance, concurrence, consonance, harmony, rapport, and tune. Idiom: meeting of the minds. Unity is also a bringing together into a whole: coalition, consolidation, unification, and union. Unity can be the results of combining: combination, composite, compound, conjugation, unification, and union. Unity is also an identity or coincidence of interests, purposes, or sympathies among the members of a group: oneness, solidarity, and union.[62]

Unity according to The Anchor Bible Dictionary is the totality of that which is diverse and varied. It is a oneness, which does not obliterate what is distinctive about its members. (Freedman, The Anchor Bible Dictionary Volume 6 Si-Z, 1992)[63] Unity does not mean uniformity, but solidarity, the tension-filled interconnection between those who differ among themselves.

Abram told Lot in Genesis 13:8-9, "Let there be no strife, I pray thee, from me: if thou wilt take the left hand, then I will go to the right; or if thou depart to the right hand, then I will go to the left."[64] Abram was determined that there was going to be unity and not war between he and Lot. Nobody at this point in this context seems to want to let unity abide, and not division, strife, or disunity. There has to be an Abram in this context that will give up his portion in order for the whole to succeed in a better way. Abram was not concerned with the, me, my, and I syndrome. He realized it was not all about him, and what he felt was the best thing to do.

---

[62] www.yourdictionary.com

[63] David Noel Freedman and others, eds., The Anchor Bible Dictionary Volume 6 Si-Z, (New York: Doubleday Publishing Group Inc., 1992) 746.

[64] Genesis 13:8-9, King James Study Bible.

Also Psalm 133:1 says, "Behold how good and how pleasant it is for brothers to dwell to together in unity!"[65] To get a better understanding of this Psalm the writer will propound a brief exegetical analysis of this text.

Textual Criticism

When this text is compared to other texts, there is not that big of a difference. Three of the texts use the Word good and only one uses the words wonderful. All of the texts use the word pleasant. However, only three keep the word brothers, while one text differs by using the word kindred. Three of the texts use the word unity while only one uses the word harmony.

The word that this project is centered around is unity. In the context of Grace Paradise Fellowship Baptist Church, the Black community is divided and there is not much progress being made that is going to benefit everyone. In this area, there are mainly middle-class American families, The non-Anglo population in this area is 26%.[66] That is only six points less than the average of what it is in the United States. This number shows that the African American voice is not strong because of the number of non-African- American people living in this area. When change is needed, numbers are important. One does not have a voice if he cannot produce the numbers. Numbers also equal buying power and therefore one has a greater voice. Jeffery often wondered why issues

---

[65] Psalm 133:1 King James Study Bible.

[66] http://www.link2lead.com

pertaining to the Black Community were often overlooked in this context and now he understands why. It is of the uttermost importance that the Black communities in this town come together and make their voice be heard. Moreover, this will take a unified front; it cannot come from two or three voices only, it has to come from the majority of the Black voices.

Form Criticism

Psalm 133:1 is in the form of a song. It is a song of Ascents of David according to The Maxwell Leadership Bible New King James Version[67] and the Layman's Parallel Bible.[68] According to the *NIV Matthew Henry Commentary*, this Psalm is a brief eulogy on unity and brotherly love. (Gerald, 1992)[69] Eulogy here applies to a prepared speech or writing extolling the virtues and services of a person.[70]

Source Criticism

Some conjure that David penned this Psalm on the occasion of the union between the tribes when they all met unanimously to make him king. It is a Psalm of general use to all societies, smaller and larger, civil, and sacred. According to modem scholarship, there is no reason for depriving David of the authorship of this sparkling sonnet. He knew by

---

[67] Psalm 133:1 The Maxwell Leadership Bible, 2002.

[68] Psalm 133:1 The Layman's Parallel Bible.

[69] Peter Gerald, *In One Volume the NIV Matthew Henry Commentary*, (Grand Rapids: Zondervan Publishing House, 1992), 749.

[70] www.yourdictionary.com.

experience the bitterness occasioned by divisions in families and was well prepared to celebrate in choicest Psalmody the blessing of unity for which he sighed. Among the "Songs of Degrees," this hymn has certainly attained unto a good degree, and even in common literature it is frequently quoted for its perfume and dew. In this Psalm there is no worry world, all is "sweetness and light," -- a notable ascent from Psalm 110 with which the Pilgrims set out. This is full of war and lamentation, but this sings of peace and pleasantness. The visitors to Zion were about to return, and this may have been their hymn of joy because they had seen such union among the tribes who had gathered at the common altar. The previous Psalm, which sings of the covenant, had also revealed the center of Israel's unity in the Lord's anointed and the promises made to him. No wonder brethren dwell in unity when God dwells among them and finds his rest in them. Translators have given to this Psalm an admirable explanatory heading, "The benefit of the communion of saints." These good persons often hit off the meaning of a passage in a few words.[71] There was division but now there is unity. Because of this example from David, Jeffery now feels a sense of comfort that unity is possible and attainable.

Contextualization

Psalm 133 helps to shed light on the meaning and need for unity. The context of Grace Paradise is in serious need of unity. The church leaders have to come to some type of agreement that is not dealing with doctrine or sacraments in order for the community to have a greater say in what goes on

---

[71] Ibid, 37.

in areas that affect change. Ecumenical movement has to take place within this context. If one person says that a change needs to occur no one will listen, but if six hundred or seven hundred people say a change needs to occur, people will listen.

New Testament

The writer of Ephesians helps to deal with an ecumenical movement in chapter 4, verses 3-7. There are no big Ts' and little 'Yous'. The church is called into one body. In the New Testament, unity is of particular concern at two points: the unity of humanity and the unity of the Church. The unity of humanity is a concept, which was widely present in the ancient, particularly the Hellenistic, world. For Paul it was an organizing principle of his anthropology and represented in part in his response to the anthropology of his contemporaries.

The unity of the church was a burning issue for Paul, the gospel of John, and to a lesser degree the Synoptic. Bauer successfully challenged the older view of scholarship that an initial study within the Church was threatened only by the rise of later heresy in 1934. From the beginning, in fact, the church was confronted with both doctrinal and sociological disunity. (Freedman, The Anchor Bible Dictionary Volume 6 Si-Z, 1992)[72] Upon further examination of this text, prayerfully a better understanding of ecumenical unity will be brought to the light, which will continue to under gird the

---

[72] David Noel Freedman and others, eds, The Anchor Bible Dictionary Volume 6 Si-Z, (New York: Doubleday Publishing Group, Inc. 1992) 746.

writers' biblical foundation for this context.

These verses from Ephesians 4:3-7 begin to spell out what constitutes the worthy walk. Such noble conduct includes humility, patience toward others, and bending over backward to maintain unity, or harmony among God's people. When looking at the text, the writer sees that three of the texts keep the word unity and the Living Bible uses the word together which is a synonym of unity. In that regard, there is not much of a difference in the text at this point in verse four, all of the texts keep the word one in referring to the body and the hope of the calling. In verses five and six, there is not much change that has taken place in the wording of the text. In this text, the word one keeps coming to the forefront. This passage elaborates on the "unity of the Spirit" This oneness among Christians refers to having one body - the one body of Christ, the Christian church; one Spirit - the same Holy Spirit who imparts the same spiritual life to all believers; one hope- all Christians share the same future certainty and are headed toward the same heavenly destination; one Lord-all submit to the same divine ruler, Jesus; one Faith-all believers have placed the same trust in Christ for salvation; One Baptism- Holy Spirit baptism at the time of salvation one God and Father-ell believers in Christ have the same God and Heavenly Father.[73]

Form Criticism

According to the New Bible *Commentary the 21s1 Century Edition*, Ephesians is breathtaking in its theological

---

[73] Ephesians 3:1-7 *The King James Study Bible*

grasp of the scope of God's purposes in Christ for the church. It is a pastorally warm letter and spiritually sensitive in its advice, peaceable in tone and readily overflowing into joyful worship.[74]

Therefore, the author is suggesting that this epistle is in the form of a letter. *The New Jerome Biblical Commentary* and *The NIV Matthew Henry Commentary* agree that this epistle is in the form of a letter. Harper's Bible Commentary also agrees with the other commentaries that this epistle is in the form of a letter.

In the fourth chapter of Ephesians, the letter turns to exhortations to Christian duties, to mutual love, unity, and concord with proper means and motives to promote these facets of being. *The New Jerome Biblical Commentary* put it this way "At the beginning of the hortatory section, the image of Paul, the prisoner in the Lord, is again invoked to confer his authority upon the exhortations." (Others, 1968-2000)[75] The NIV- Matthew Henry Commentary says that in this passage there are various exhortations to important duties i.e., mutual love, Christian purity, and holiness of life. (Gerald, 1992)[76] The conclusion that the writer has come to is that Ephesians is in the form of a letter, and chapter four and following is filled with exhortations.

---

[74]

[75] D.A. Carson and others, eds. *New Bible Commentary 21st Century Edition*, (Leicester, England: Varsity Press) 576.

[76] Peter Gerald, *In One Volume the NIV Matthew Henry Commentary*, (Grand Rapids: Zondervan Publishing House, 1992) 629.686.

Source Criticism

This passage is redacted from 1 Corinthians 12:13, and Colossians 3:12-15. 1 Corinthians 12:13 says for by one Spirit are we baptized into one body, whether we be Jews or Gentiles, whether we be bound or free; and have been all made to drink into one Spirit. Colossians 3:12-15 says put on therefore, as the elect of God, holy and beloved, bowels of mercies, kindness, humbleness of mind, meekness, long-suffering; Forbearing one another, and forgiving one another, if any may have a quarrel against any: even as Christ forgave you, so also do ye. And above all these things put on charity, which is the bound of perfectness, and let the peace of God rule in your hearts, to the which also you are called in one body; and be ye thankful.[77] The mention of being called in one body in Colossians 3:15 leads to a seven-part statement of the pervasiveness of the unity that must characterize Christian life. The reference to unity in baptism is fitting here within the ecclesiological perspective of Ephesians.

Contextualization

Brothers and sisters, what good is a church if it cannot come together for a common goal and be united in the bounds of brotherly love? The nature of that unity is the unity of the spirit. The Christian unity is in the heart or spirit: it does not lie in one set of thoughts, nor in one form and mode of worship, but in one heart and soul. This is what the church must strive to keep. If individuals quarrel with members of the church or community, they must take all possible care not

---

[77] Ibid.

to quarrel with those who view things differently. In the context of Griffin and Spalding County where Grace Paradise is located, there is a serious need for change and unity in the Black community among the churches. How can the church affect change if it does not come together? How can the community have a greater voice if it does not come together?

Historical Traces of Unity

This discussion will start with the term ecumenical, which is a relatively new word that refers to an old phenomenon in the Christian life. This discussion will deal with this notion of the importance of reuniting separated churches. According to *The Westminster Dictionary of Christian Theology in Mediaeval Times*, there were attempts (Councils of Lyons, 1274 and Florence, 1438-1439) to bring together the Eastern and Western churches, and the first stages of the Protestant Reformation were closely followed by attempts to heal the new wounds that were brought about as a result of division. (Alan Richardson, 1983)[78]

Before the discussion goes further, the term ecumenical must be defined how this term will be used to under gird this project. According to Bruce L. Shelley in Church History in Plain Language, the word ecumenical is defined as a term that means worldwide or universal. (Shelley, 1982)[79] When applied to Christian churches it implies the oneness of

---

[78] Alan Richardson and John Bowden, *The Westminster Dictionary of Christian Theology*, (Philadelphia: The Westminster Press, 1983), 173.

[79] Bruce L. Shelley and others, eds, *Updated 2nd Edition Church History in Plain Language*, (Dallas: Word Publishing, 1982) 442.

Christians in the faith wherever they may be found. The oneness is what is missing in this context. There is a lot of division that has to be addressed for the good of the people. The writer understands that there are many roadblocks and differences in the various denominations, but a common ground is essential at this point for survival.

This unity can either be a spiritual reality apart from organizations of men – as evangelicals are inclined to argue- or an effort to create some federations of churches or some merger of denominations. The voices of time past, says Shelley, call the spirit of unity "ecumenicity" and the organizational effort the "ecumenical movement."[80]

After the Reformation, however, the word slipped into relative oblivion, and it is only within recent decades that it has returned to popular usage. That usage has to center more and more on a concern among divided Christians for unity. The Oxford Conference on the Life and Work of the Church (1937), attended by both Protestant and Orthodox theologians, stated in its report that "The Churches" are ecumenical in so far as they attempt to realize the Una Sancta, the Fellowship of Christians who acknowledge one Lord." (McAfee, 1969)[81]

That old word from the Greek was reborn and brought back into circulation, along with the fundamental idea for which it stood in the early Christian centuries the idea of the

---

[80] Ibid.

[81] Brown Robert McAfee, *Ecumenical Revolution an Interpretation of the Catholic*.

whole household of faith."[82] Upon further digging, the writer found that all of the English derivatives, such as ecumenical, ecumenicity, ecumenices, and ecumenism, are simply transliterations from the Greek work oikumene. (For this reason, says Brown, British theologians, linguistically purer than their North American barbarian cousin, frequently refer to oecumenicity, the oecumenical movement, and so forth.) The original Greek word as used by Herodotus was innocent of any theological overtones.

In its turn it derives from oikos, meaning house or dwelling (and, by extension, household, or family) and from this comes the verb oikeo, to live or dwell. From the present passive particle of the verb comes oikoumene, which means the land where people live or dwell and comes in time to describe "the inhabited earth." For the Greeks, the word describes the Greek world; for the Romans, the term was equated with the Roman Empire.[83]

According to the Westminster Dictionary the theologically neutral word, however, begins to have theological, or at least ecclesiastical, overtones in the early centuries of the church. It is used to describe, for example, something pertaining to the whole of the church, i.e., to the church wherever it is in "the inhabited world." (Alan Richardson, the Westminster Dictionary of christian Theology, 1983)[84] Oikos is household or home. Home is

---

[82] Ibid.

[83] Ibid.

[84] Alan Richardson and John Bowden, The Westminster Dictionary of Christian Theology, (Philadelphia: The Westminster Press, 1983), 173.

where people know your name. Home is where they can tell your story and therefore oikic becomes work to make the world into a home. How can the church be prepared to serve God's oikic work in this context?

Soon it becomes customary to speak of the ecumenical council as those at which the church had representation from all parts of the inhabited world. Even by 381 A.D. the council of Constantinople could refer to Nicaea as an ecumenical synod. Eastern Orthodoxy today calls ecumenical only those seven church councils occurring before the great schism of 1054 A.D. Roman Catholics, believing that the fullness of the means of salvation can be obtained only by those in communion with the See of Rome, call subsequent councils, such as Trent and Vatican I, at which the Catholic Church was represented, ecumenical councils.

It is thus consistent with Roman Catholic usage to refer to Vatican II as an ecumenical council, though neither Orthodox nor Protestants would feel the term descriptively accurate since, from their perspective, the church was not present.) (McAfee, 1969)[85] The word ecumenical came to be more and more frequently used to describe the yearning of Christians to recover the unity they had obscured by their divisions. However, Oliver Tompkins, long active in the World Council, has stated, "The word ecumenical is used to denote interest in Christian unity and church union."[86]

Bernard Lambert defined ecumenism as this he said "It is

---

[85] Robert McAfee Brown, Ecumenical Revolution an Interpretation of the Catholic Protestant Dialogue, (Garden City, New York: Doubleday & Company, Inc. 1967) 193.

[86] Ibid.

a mystique, a method, a mode of action. Thus, it supplies a universal need." Bernard goes on to say that the Word denotes the inhabited surface of the globe and whatever relates to it. (Lambert, 1967)[87] Lastly, the phrase designates the awareness of belonging to a world of Christian fellowship and indicates a desire for union with other churches. This final meaning dates from the first twenty years of the nineteenth century when it was used as an explanation of the presence of representatives of many different churches at the conferences of Stockholm and Lausanne. It was continued in the Oxford Conference of 1937.[88]

This dialogue enables the churches to come together and hold discussions in order to reach agreement on the measures to be taken with reunion of the churches as the goal. So the phrase "ecumenical movement" denotes an immense activity undertaken by every Christian community, which by means of dialogue, co-operation, integration, and individual and institutional union aims at drawing Christians together and reconciling them, healing, their damaged traditions, and in short, bringing the mystical Body of Christ to its perfect fulfillment.[89] To be involved in ecumenism means being involved in the totality of ideas, principles, problems, activities, and institutions which together account for the origin and development of the ecumenical movement.

The *Dictionary of Theology* put it this way, "The

---

[87] Bernard Lambert, *Ecumenism Theology and History,* (New York: Herder and Herder, 1967) 29.

[88] Ibid.

[89] Ibid.

ecumenical movement has the charter of authentic dialogue, which is fundamentally a conversation oriented towards an open future. It is not a question of approaching other church communities as such, nor is it simply a return on the part of the non-Catholic churches to the Catholic Church."[90] The theme of ecumenical dialogue is everything that can be of service to the unity of Christians in faith, church, Christian life, and responsible action with regard to overcome real doctrinal differences and arrangements for shared activities. To further deal with this notion of dialogue, Robert MacAfee Brown wrote an article on the subject of from diatribe to dialogue and Hooft and Bea came along and strengthened his arguments. Their discussion helps add strength to this discussion.

Why should the churches in this context be concerned with this ecumenical movement? Bea and Hooft are of the opinion that Ecumenism stems from love; but love does not rejoice at wrong, but rejoices in the right (I Corinthians 13:4) (Cardinal Augustine Bea, 1967)[91]

The ecumenical movement had been started by the Protestant and Anglican churches in Europe and North America, and by the Greek-speaking Orthodox Churches. At that time, the churches of Asia and Africa were not yet autonomous. The churches of Russia were completely cut off from the rest of the world. Shortly before the Second World War, the churches in Asia and Africa began to play an active

---

[90] Karl Rahner and Vorgimler Herbert, *Dictionary of Theology*, (New York: The Crossroad Publishing Company), 1965. 144

[91] Cardinal Augustine Bea and Hooft Willem Visser't, Peace Among Christians, (New York: Herder and Herder Association Press, 1967), 23.

part in the movement. Their main contributions came after they became independent and autonomous.

The writer has thus reached one of the aims set up by the pioneers of the ecumenical movement. All the Christian churches are to enter into conversation with each other, they are no longer to live in isolation, they are to realize that the cause of Christ transcends the boundaries of their own institutional life; they are to discover their solidarity, to cooperate in common task, and to seek together for ways which lead to full unity. Henceforth all the churches are obliged to get to know one another. They are making discoveries. They are astonished to answer the question put to them by their sister churches. They have to rethink many positions, which are no longer in accordance with the new situation, to formulate them afresh or even to revise them.[92] The message of the Stockholm Conference in 1925 said "The nearer we come to the crucified Christ, the nearer we come to one another." The whole life of the ecumenical movement shows that the church can make progress only by carefully studying the Gospel of Jesus Christ together.[93]

The ecumenical movement is directed towards reestablishing this peace among the churches, toward leading them back to a unity of the spirit through the bond of peace. Modras in his book Path to unity said "strictly speaking the ecumenical movement is defined as the effort and activity of Christians in various churches to promote the restoration of Christian unity. By establishing relationships between

---

[92] Ibid.

[93] Ibid.

Christian Churches, the ecumenical movement seeks to heal the schisms, i.e., the formal separations, which divided them one from another. In practice it consists of the efforts of both individual Christians and Christian Churches to help one another become more Christ like to realize more fully the Christian ideal after which they all strive." (Modras, 1968)[94]

It was the moral cancer of racial discrimination, which first brought ecumenism in the United States out of the calm logic of theological discussion and into the sweaty thick of the picket line. Catholics, Protestants, Orthodox, Jews, and secular humanist banded together in trying to overcome discrimination in housing, employment, health, education, and the administration of justice.

Regardless of economic condition, or color someone has to come against the exploitation of the various evils in the community. The vastness and complexity of society today, however, is such that only a united voice raised by all humankind of good will and can prick the conscience of this age.[95] According to Ellingsen in 1948, immediately following World War II, the ecumenical movement especially the World Council of Churches (WCC), came to fruition after decades of preparatory work. Helped by Vatican II's ecumenical impulses, the WCC has overseen some exciting strides to unity, most notably the so-called Lima Text a 1982 consensus statement of representatives of the member churches on Baptism, Eucharist, and Ministry. (Ellingsen,

---

[94] Ronald Modras, Paths to Unity American Religion Today and Tomorrow, (New York: Sheet and Ward. 1968) 9.

[95] Ibid.

1999)[96]

However, as the twenty-first century dawned, it has been generally by most ecumenical organizations that the vision of unity that should be pursued is interdenominational (a situation in which denominations would preserve their distinct characteristics but their difference would be understood as reconciled.) As such these distinctions are to be seen as not divisive but a witness to the diversity of the biblical witness. Given this new ecumenical vision of unity, it would be possible for denominations to make binding decisions together for a greater good.

For the sake of this discussion a working definition by the writer of the term ecumenical will not be as broad and loosely used as this term has been used in the past. Ecumenical Unity in this context will be defined as unity that seeks to reconnect the African American church and community in this context through the paradigm of multilateral ecumenical unity no matter their denomination for a greater cause that will seek to create a greater voice in this context or oikos. In hopes that the pastor and church will partner together to renew the community.

Ecumenical Unity involves economy, ecology and oikoumene, economy – will everyone in the oikos (household) have access to what it takes to live and live abundantly. Ecology- will nature have an oikos (home) its own living space, and oikoumene- will the peoples of earth be able to inhabit the earth in peace. Therefore, oikoumene then takes in not just the unity of the Church but God's oikic work

---

[96] Mark Ellingsen, Reclaiming Our Roots an Inclusive Introduction to Church History (Harrisburg, PA: Trinity Press International, 1999) 235.

to make the world into a home. If unity is the road that will lead to change why not take that road even if it has not been taken before. Unity that will affect change is the ultimate goal of this project. The topic of discussion does not just deal with multilateral ecumenical unity it becomes multilateral oikoumene unity, which becomes multilateral oikic unity to establish God's work to make the world into a home within this context.

Chapter 4: Methodology

The hypothesis for this work is that if the churches come together and work together, the communities will have a stronger voice. The leaders of the churches in this context are not united. The churches are not united. Consequently, the community is suffering because of the divisions.

The project focus group came from members of the Grace Paradise Fellowship Baptist Church located at 1980 Futural Road in Griffin, Georgia. Letters were distributed after worship service to all of the members of Grace Paradise asking them would they like to participate in the focus group for this project. Jeffery learned that if internal unity has not been dealt with then external unity will not be achieved. Hence the writer began internally initially and then progressed outward.

There were eight people who said they would participate in the project. Those eight people were first given a pretest (see appendix h) to see how much they already knew about ecumenical unity and the community. After the pre-test was administered, those participants participated in Bible Study (see appendix b and to learn about unity from a Biblical perspective. They also listened to a sermon series on various subjects dealing with unity (see appendixes d-f) to gain further clarification about unity. After each sermon, they were given questions about the sermon to answer to see if their understanding about unity had been strengthened (see appendix g). Finally, they were given a post-test to demonstrate their comprehensive understanding of ecumenical unity.

One concept Jeffery learned from this project is that *unity* is possible, and that people in the community want to fellowship. The writer also learned that some of the leaders in this context want to fellowship and work together to make the community better.

Chapter 5: Field Experience

The object of this project was to establish a connection between the church and community through ecumenical unity. The African American voice in this context was not being taken seriously. The writer felt that unity was the only way to get the numbers needed to foster change in this context. What better place to start than with the leaders of the community and the pastor of the churches in this area. The visibility of the pastor working together will make a difference in the community. It is not about denominations, sacraments, or days of worship, but the real issue is what is being done to make a difference in the communities that are being served. Holy Scripture describes love as the bond that binds everything together. Thus, the church must be seen as a community of mutual love, which functions as an essential expression of unity.

Data for this project was collected using a pre-test, a post-test, and critical analysis of questions from a sermon series. This model will hopefully serve as an example for other areas and communities as they seek to bridge the gap that exists between the church and community.

The results from the questions from the sermon series are as follows. As one can imagine, the response to each question had a variety of responses from the persons answering the questions. The subject for this sermon was "Unity for What." The Biblical reference was John 17:21. This sermon was preached on September 10, 2006.

The first question asked was "Did this sermon impact your thinking about unity in a negative or positive way?" One participant responded, "This sermon made me think in a positive way about how we need to come together as one. We need to stand up for our brothers and sisters and not just sit back and do nothing. We need to support each other." Respondent two answered this question this way. "This sermon impacted my thinking about unity in a positive way because we all need to come together as one."

Respondent three answered this question this way. "The sermon impacted my thinking in a very profound and positive way. We all need to come together and work as one body with one vision." Respondent four answered this question this way. "This sermon impacted me in a positive way because we need to be one in the church. There are no little I's and big you's in this ministry." Respondent five answered this question this way. "This sermon impacted my thinking in a positive way based on the fact that we as African Americans are so divided in our home, schools, churches, and the community. This sermon brought out the fact that we need to pull together as a race and support one another."

Respondent six answered this question this way. "This sermon impacted my thinking in a positive way. Churches, communities, and other places need to be unified. The world and the people have lost their sense of the purpose of unity." Respondent seven answered this question this Way. "This sermon impacted my thinking in a positive way because, people are hurting, beat down, destroyed, and there are a lot of lost souls because of disunity. We must come together as one, one body with one spirit"

Respondent eight answered this question this way. "This sermon impacted my thinking in a positive way. It brings home the point that God expressed unity, and if we are going to walk in Christ, we must align ourselves completely with his word and teachings."

The second question asked was has your understanding of unity changed since hearing this sermon? Respondent one answered this question this way: "Yes I am clearer on what unity is. I now have a better understanding of the total concept of unity as a whole."

Respondent two answered this question this way: "Yes my understanding of unity has changed; this sermon taught me that we all need to be on one accord." Respondent three answered this question this way: "Yes this sermon has changed my understanding about unity. I am more than willing, ready, and able to voice my opinion on matters of importance in my community."

Respondent four answered this question this way: "Yes this sermon has changed my opinion about unity."

Respondent five answered this question this way: "Yes this sermon has changed my opinion about unity. I now realize that unity no longer just involves my inner circle. However, unity involves others in my community that I may or may not directly know."

Respondent six answered this question this way: "My understanding of unity has expanded since hearing this sermon."

Respondent seven answered this question this way: "No my understanding of unity has not changed because unity has been in my spirit for a while."

Respondent eight answered this question this way: "This sermon confirmed and have more validity to what I know about unity. I feel better equipped to help bring about change in my community."

The third question asked was what areas about unity were focused on in this sermon? All the persons who answered the questions were in agreement that this sermon focused on being one in our community, church, schools, and family except one who said the sermon focus was on "Black people" coming together and taking a stand.

The fourth question for this sermon was did this sermon move you to take action to unify an area in our community? Respondent one responded to this question in this manner: "Yes this sermon caused me to want to take action. If there is something going on that I can make a difference in, I want to be more involved."

Respondent two answered this question this way: "Yes this sermon moved me to want to take action in a positive way to help make my community better."

Responded three answered this question this way: Yes, this sermon moved me to pray more for our school system and children in the community. I learned that unity would benefit everyone not just me."

Respondent four answered this question this way: "Yes this sermon caused me to want to be more vocal about concerns in the community. We need to speak up more for each other."

Respondent five answered this question this way: "Yes this sermon made me more aware of the fact that we can make a difference together. I must remember to stand up for my fellow man and support them as they support me."

Respondent six answered to question four was as follows: "This sermon has moved me to action to enlighten people in the community about coming together not only when things affect them but to stand together when others need assistance as well."

Respondent seven answered this question this way: "The church has an awesome responsibility to come together for the sake of carrying out the gospel message. If the members work together, we can have a greater effect on the community."

Responded eight answered this question this way: "Yes this sermon moved me to action in the schools. This sermon caused me to be aware of the fact how unity affects our kids. We need to come together to make sure the kids are being singled out or stereotyped for the wrong reasons."

The subject for this sermon was "Watering Parched Places." The Bible references that this sermon centered around was Psalm 133. It was preached September 17, two-thousand six. Each person's response will be listed after each question.

The first question was, "Did this sermon impact your thinking about unity in a negative or positive way?" Respondent one said, "The sermon did impact my thinking about unity in a positive way. Unity is a vital part of our lives. It impacts the individual family, and communities. Respondent one said it impacts the way we think and the ability to help others."

Respondent two answered question one this way. "This sermon impacted my thinking in a very positive way. It made me want to go out and help my community."

Respondent three answered question two this way. "We all need to come together as one."

Respondent four answered question one this way. "This sermon impacted my thinking in a positive way. It justified the fact that the church is God existing in the community."

Respondent five answered question one this way. "This sermon impacted my thinking in a positive way. It's always encouraging to hear a sermon that will make you want to move to action."

Respondent six answered question one this way. "Yes, it impacted my life in a positive way because if you are not one body in Christ you are lost"

Respondent seven answered question one this way. "This sermon impacted my thinking about unity in a positive way because we should be unified throughout the community and not just in the church."

The second question that was asked was, "Has your understanding of unity changed since hearing this sermon? Respondent one answered this question this way. "No, I am still able to realize the importance of unity. It is not possible for one individual alone with no other help to make a positive effect on the community, churches, and homes. It takes all the interested participants to focus on the vital parts of a situation and unite together to determine the outcome they are seeking."

Respondent two answered the question this way. "Yes, my understanding about unity has changed since hearing this sermon. I am more encouraged because of the effect unity can have in my household, my church, and community. I also feel more compassion for others and their well-being."

Respondent three answered the question this way. "Yes, my understanding of unity has changed since hearing this sermon a whole lot"

Respondent four answered this question this way. "My understanding of unity after hearing this sermon has grown tremendously."

Respondent five answered this question this way. "After hearing this sermon, I am able to see how unity canoe put into action in this community on a greater scale."

Respondent six answered this question this way. "Yes, my understanding of unity has changed since hearing this sermon because my way of thinking about unity has changed. My thoughts are no longer the same as before. I now have a far greater understanding of unity."

Respondent seven answered the question this way. "Yes, my understanding has changed since hearing this sermon about Psalm 133. My understanding is no longer just about our church, but we have to reach out to others as well."

The third question asked was what areas about unity were focused on in this sermon? Responded one said, "Unity starts from the head which consists of the leaders of various organizations and churches. These leaders must unite and come together for a greater cause than their own. The power or impact of unity then focuses on the members and others. Unity starts from the top and runs down to each individual."

Respondent two answered this question this way. "The unity of the family, Church, and community."

Respondent three answered this question this way. "This sermon focused on being together as one, with one voice."

Respondent four answered this question this way, "This sermon focused on the board of education, the community, and the world around us in general."

Respondent five answered this question this way. "This sermon focused on how individuals should continue the unity that was started by Christ"

Respondent six answered this question this way. "We should unify with others to make a difference for the children."

Respondent seven answered this question this way. "The sermon focused on our community and families."

The fourth question for this sermon was did this sermon move you to take action to unify an area in our community? Explain. Respondent one answered this question this way. "Yes, I work in a school where the majority of our race is divided and others are trying desperately to keep us divided, and down. Daily my task is to uplift others with the power to succeed to their fullest and increase unity."

Respondent two answered this question this way. "Yes, this sermon has caused me to focus more on our young people."

Respondent three answered this question this way_ "Yes we as a race need to come together and speak out about things that are happening in our community"

Respondent four answered this question this way. "This sermon moved. me to take action toward the youth in the community and not only the ones in the church,"

Respondent five answered this question this way. "Yes, this moved me to want to take action in our school system so that the children today will be prepared to run our country and share these efforts with likeminded Christians. This sermon reminds one of a conversation that I had with a friend a few weeks ago. She asked did I know the difference between a Muslim in a community that is failing and a Christian. She said that the main difference is that a Christian will watch people selling drugs and carrying guns around and a Muslim will walk up to them and take the drugs and gun. If we could bring in the Muslim ideas into our faith, we would be better equipped to deal with controversy and address disunity."

Respondent six answered this question this way. "This sermon moved me to action because the community as a whole need to come together to make it better for the little ones of tomorrow."

Respondent seven answered this question this way. " Yes, this sermon moved me to action with those in a leadership position. If we do not have good examples to follow, then we will continue to do what we have always done."

The writer also preached a sermon entitled isn't that Good News. The sermon was preached on September 24, 2006, at Grace Paradise Fellowship Baptist Church in Griffin, Georgia. The scripture reference for this sermon came from Ephesians 4:3-6. The sermon can be found in the appendix in its entirety (see appendix F). The results from that sermon are as follows: The first question asked was did this sermon impact your thinking about unity in a negative or positive way? Respondent one answered this question this way, "This sermon impacted my thinking in a positive way about unity because the churches, schools, and communities are lacking unity. They want to take individual credit for God's work."

Respondent two also said that this sermon impacted his thinking in a positive way. Their response was "Through Christ we (the churches, members, and community) are a body of one. When one member is in need, we are all in need."

Respondent three also agreed with the other two that this sermon impacted his thinking in a positive way. Respondent four said this sermon showed how Christ expects us to be unified.

Respondent six said that this sermon impacted his thinking about unity in a positive way. It also made him more concerned about the local school system and our kids. He now realizes that unity affects everyone.

The next question was, "Has your understanding of unity changed since hearing this sermon?" Responded one said, "My thinking has changed about unity. I now know more about unity and what it can do for my community."

Respondent two agreed that their understanding about unity has changed. They are now more concerned about things and the people around them. Their exact words were, "I am sometimes that person that drives through the community refusing to notice what is around me and affecting my community. I am now more aware of my surroundings."

Respondent three agrees with the other two about the fact that this sermon has helped to change their understanding about unity. Their overall concern is whether or not the members of Grace are on one accord or not.

Respondent four agrees that their understanding about unity has changed. They said that this sermon revealed to them that you have to go beyond your everyday surroundings and try to help others.

Respondent five says that you have to care more about others in the community. Unity affects everyone, not just a select group of individuals. Question three was what areas about unity were focused on in this sermon?

Respondent one's answer was, "The areas concerning unity focused on in this sermon were the churches, schools, and communities. Regardless of what church we belong to, we all should be on one accord for God's kingdom."

Respondent two answered this question this way, "We are one through Christ's death burial and resurrection. The leaders are not leading the community. We need to join forces and unite. The community's awareness about concerns needs to be increased so problems that concern us can be addressed in a timely manner."

Respondent three said that the sermon was about everyone being on one accord.

Respondent four said that the sermon's main focus was on the leaders and them stepping up and being the leader that God has called them to be.

Respondent five said that the sermon focused on the various schools, and it was about the high school dropout rate. The last question that was addressed was did this sermon move you to take action to unify an area in our community? Explain. Respondent one answered this question this way. "This sermon has moved me to take more action with the youth in the community because if you start with them when they are young, when they get old, they can teach others about the love of God."

Respondent two answered this question this way, they said I need to go outside of my comfort zone and help others,"

Respondent three said, "Yes, this sermon did move me to take action to unify an area in our community because we all need to come together and help others make this world a better place."

Respondent four answered this question this way, "Yes, this sermon moved me to take action to unify an area in my community namely the school system, because our school system needs improvement" Respondent five also said that this sermon also made them to want to help more in our school system."

The writer also taught several Bible lessons on unity and

the importance of unity (See appendix). The primary focus of the Bible lessons was to give strong Biblical support for a Biblical understanding of unity.

After the Bible lessons and sermon series, the writer did a post-test to see had any of the people's understanding about unity changed or did their thinking about unity stay the same. The results of the post-test are as follows.

The data suggests that unity is possible and that the people in this context want a unified community. The data also suggests that if the churches come together, it will have a great impact on our children and most importantly our community. The data suggests lastly that unity in this context will produce the needed numbers fax change and a strong voice.

Chapter 6: Reflection, Summary, and Conclusion

The writer's aim for this project was to understand or come to some type of conclusion concerning the lack of unity in Griffin and Spalding County. The title was born out of the premise that there could be a bridging of the gap between church and community. The question that had to be asked and pondered upon was what would it take to reconnect the church and community? Therefore, the title was not only born, but it was also starting to live out a reality that was much needed in this context. The title for this project is Reconnecting the Church and Community through Multilateral Ecumenical Unity: The Church Speaking as One Voice with One Purpose.

For the sake of this discussion, a working definition by the writer of the term ecumenical was not used as broad and loosely as this term has been used in the past. Ecumenical Unity in this context was defined as unity that seeks to reconnect the African American church and community in this context through the paradigm of multilateral ecumenical unity no matter their denomination for a greater cause that will seek to create a greater voice in this context or oikos. The hope is that the pastors and churches will collaborate to renew the community and speak truth to power. The increase in visibility was a focal point of this project. The churches have been in hiding far as the writer was concerned and this projects aim was to bring them out of their shells and back into the light. Our job essentially is to let our light shine. Being a drum major for justice causes lights to shine like never before.

The topic of discussion did not just deal with multilateral ecumenical unity it became multilateral oikoumene unity, which became multilateral oikic, which is unity to establish God's work to make the world into a home within this context. After all, the whole world is Our hospital.

This project taught the writer first and foremost that unity is absent in many areas in the community and that lack of unity is affecting the communities' ability to move forward. The main issue with churches in this area is that they are focused solely on internal growth and development and not worried about external wholeness. There has to be a balance between our in reach and outreach.

This project also showed the writer that many people in this context are eager to come together and help make Griffin and Spalding County better. The areas that the research showed would benefit the most from a unifying effort by everyone in this Context are the schools, our children, our communities, and our churches. Regardless of economic condition, or color someone has to come against the exploitation of the various evils in the community. The vastness and complexity of society today, however, is such that only a united voice raised by all humankind of goodwill can prick the conscience of our age and this is what this project did.

The methods that were used in this project were a pre-questionnaire, sermon series, post-sermon questions, bible study, and post-questionnaire. These methods demonstrated that the majority of the people does have a heighten awareness and appreciation concerning unity. Since this project began there have been more interest in the leaders in the community coming together to foster change in the community. A large community rally took place while this project was in the early stages. That rally centered on a controversy at City Hall in Griffin. That rally let the city official and county official know that the people of Griffin and Spalding County were not going to be overlooked and that our voices were going to be heard at all costs or by any means necessary.

Some things that could have been done differently were that more community leaders could have been involved sooner in the project and more attention could have been given to issues in the community. The more people that are involved the better the outcome will be for everyone.

This project has helped the writer grow in his understating about community development.

Dr. J. A. Gladney

Grassroots Unifier

Rev. Walter C. James is the Pastor Emeritus of the Eight St. Baptist Church in Griffin, Georgia. Pastor James has been active in this context for over twenty-five years, served on numerous committees and he has spoken truth to power as long as I can remember. One of the reasons why he was contacted for this project is because he served as the president of the Ministers Union during one of its more active periods.

He so vividly talked about how the Ministers Union was very instrumental in getting a Street in Griffin named after Dr. Martin Luther King Jr. He also spoke of how active the ministers were at School Board Meetings and the City Council meeting and how they were behind a movement that caused change and was a voice in the community.

Dr. Lacy, the Pastor of the Mt Zion Baptist Church in Griffin Georgia, was very instrumental in training ministers at the local Ministers Union. Therefore, the Ministers Union served as a place of fellowship, a training session, and a time of sharing for the pastors.

Pastor James, however, had a somber look on his face when he was asked what he felt lead to the demise of such a movement in a time when it is still very much needed. His reply was the Ministers Union lost momentum because of a lack of support and the preachers stop coming. There also was a lack of a common interest among those participating. He said he did not really know why, but there was a lack of interest.

The discussion moved to how he felt a new movement could enhance this project and more importantly the context of Griffin and Spalding County. One thing we both agreed upon whole-heartedly is that leadership is needed to bring everyone within this context back together.

The churches need to see their leaders united. The communities need to see the ministers united and those in power need to see the ministers united. Some might say unite for what? There are several reasons for unity one reason is because there are numerous new pastors in this context, and they have no way of being introduced to key people and be given important information that could really help their ministry. A strong Ministers Union could serve as such a place to introduce new pastors to Griffin.

Another reason is to have a place where all pastors can receive the necessary training and skills, they need to hold the office of Pastor with integrity and the way God intended. It is a known fact that everyone has not had the opportunity to go to school and receive such knowledge and a Ministers Union could serve as such a place. Another reason is to help pastors become aware of benefits that are available for them that they may not be aware of.

The National Association for the Advancement of Colored People is on the decline, crime is on the rise, single parents' homes are at an all-time high and morality in the black community is at an all-time low. Therefore, God is calling those who have the mantle placed upon them to lead the people that God love so much. But let judgment run down as waters, and righteousness as a mighty stream.[97]

---

[97] Amos 5:24 King James Version

A Glimpse of Unity from God's Lips

Red Oak Grove M B Church
September 15, 2013
Text: Genesis 11:6
Pericope: Genesis 11:1-9
Subject: A Glimpse of Unity from God's Lips
Behavioral Purpose: to move hears to come together to do God's will!
Dr. J. A. Gladney

Aesop, the famous writer of fables penned a narrative about a hungry lion and four oxen. The lion would often attempt to perpetrate an attack upon the oxen at the moment when they would congregate in the open filed. However, the lion soon found that one lion proved no match for the united oxen.

It happened that on a certain day the lion found each of the oxen standing separate from each other due to a quarrel that developed among the oxen. Now it became an easy matter for the lion to pick off the oxen one-by-one. Aesop's moral to the story was that unity results in strength and division leads to failure. In other words, together we stand divided we fall.

Unity is like learning to play on a team together. "At one point during a game, the coach said to one of his young players, "Do you understand what cooperation is? What a team is?"

The little boy nodded in the affirmative. "Do you understand that what matters is whether we win together as a team." The little boy nodded yes. "So," the coach continued, "When a strike is called, or you're out at first, you don't argue or curse or attack the umpire. Do you understand all that?"

Again, the little boy nodded. "Good," said the coach. "Now go over there and explain it to your father."

The Greek word for unity is okic, which means God's work to make the world into a home. Allow me to say that God has always been for the church being on one accord. John 17:21 says That they all may be one; Psalms 133:1 says Behold, how good and how pleasant it is
for brethren to dwell together in unity! Romans 12:5 says So we, being many, are one body in Christ, and everyone members one of another. Acts 2:1 says and when the day of Pentecost was fully come, they were all with one accord in one place. As a matter of fact, Ignatius of Antioch one of the early church fathers said that it was that lack of unity that made humanity so vulnerable to the forces of evil.

The devil can easily pull the church apart if we are not on one accord. Whenever there are cliques in the house the house will always be divided. T D. Jakes gave Bishop Eddie Long a statue for one of his birthdays, this statue sits outside of Eddie Long doorway to his office. The statue captures the battle of David and Goliath, it has David holding a sword in one hand and Goliath heads in the other hand. The statue symbolizes that there is only one head in this house.

How many of you know that anything with two heads is a monster? If there is no clearly defined leader the people don't know who to follow and who's voice to listen to. That is why The Lord gives the church pastors who the church will know whose voice to follow. Jesus said in John 10:27 My sheep hear my voice, and I know them, and they follow me:

Every TV preacher, pastor, book writer, or evangelist has not been called to speak into your life if you are a part of a church body. The pastor or leader of that church body is commissioned by God to speak into and over your life. I have developed my life work to the cause of unity in the church and the community. I believe that the church does not live-in isolate apart from the community, but it works better when the church and community is on one accord.

I wrote a document some time ago entitled "Reconnecting the Local church and Community through Multilateral ecumenical unity: The church speaking as one voice with one purpose." I believe that There is this disconnect in the community that has only added to the problems of racism, police brutality, the rise of gang violence, and society taking advantage of our black women, that is fueled by our lack of unity.

When community leaders, and church leaders, are at odds caught up over a power trip mentality, who is going to get the credit, who is going to be the leader, whose name are the people going to be calling, it destroys the fabric of the community and now the police can beat up our black boys while walking, justice court judges can throw the book at our youth rather than provide treatment for them, they find any and every way to lock them up, and the system goes unchallenged because of our lack of unity.

There is this text in the Old Testament found in the book of Genesis that I think can help heal the church and allow the church to get on one accord. It is the story of the Tower of Babel. It is not my intent to look at the actions surrounding the incident of the tower, but to look at what God said concerning the people who built the tower.

Etymologically speaking (etymology is the study of words) the word Babel means the gate of God, because Bab means gate and El means god, thus Bab-el means the gate of

God. This tower that was thought to be so majestic and its heights reach heaven still fell short of the height of God, because in the initial building plans in verse four their tower top was to reach the heaven, in verse five it says The Lord left heaven and came down to see the city and its tower, which the mortals had built.

Notice at first glance it would appear that God was mad at the building project and the success of the building project. But that is not the issue, the issue with God is, the motive of the people and the people leaving God out of their plans. Look at the wording of their speech in verse four: Genesis 11:4 And they said, go to, let us build us a city and a tower, whose top may reach unto heaven; and let us make us a name, lest we be scattered abroad upon the face of the whole earth.

Anytime your plans are about us and not about God they want work. You can't ever do anything in life without God especially trying to do things that will only build you up and make a name for yourself without the help and direction of The Lord. So, the text says in verse seven that The Lord confused the people languages. I will deal with that another day, but The Lord says some of the most profound words about unity in verse six that will bless the church if we pay close attention to them. The first things that The Lord said in verse six is they are one people.

There were no big I's or little you U's the people were one. There was no confusion they were all on one accord. The bible says in Ephesians 4:4-6 these words "There is one body, and one Spirit, even as ye are called in one hope of your calling; One Lord, one faith, one baptism, One God and Father of all, who is above all, and through all, and in you all.

The church is not or should not be divided but it should

be one. The choir can't do its own thing if it's part of the one church. The deacons can't go their own way if they are part of the one church. The ushers can't stand apart from the church if they are part of the one church. No ministry of the church can operate apart from the church if it is part of the one church. The members in the pew can't function how they want to function if they are part of the one church.

1 Corinthians 12:13 For by one Spirit are we all baptized into one body, whether we be Jews or Gentiles, whether we be bond or free; and have been all made to drink into one Spirit. What good are we if we can't work together and come together to do the Lord's will.

Martin Luther king jr. said everybody has a drum major instinct in them, but the problem with that is that everybody wants to march to the beat of their own drum instead of marching together to one beat, the beat of God's drum.

Not only did God say they are one people, but he also said they all have one language: this suggest to me the people were not contradiction one another when the leader said one thing, they were all in agreement of that one thing, there was no confusion.

In The movie *Drum line,* the bands motto was One Band, One Sound. A part of Red Oak Groves motto should be one church, one sound.

1 Corinthians 1:10 says Now I beseech you, brethren, by the name of our Lord Jesus Christ, that ye all speak the same thing, and that there be no divisions among you; but that ye be perfectly joined together in the same mind and in the same judgment.

If everybody is saying the same thing the devil can't come in and divide us. The problem starts when small groups get together and start saying different stuff and then confusion comes in.

If the church agrees on it whether you like it or not it should become the language of the church. One Church-One Sound. The churches greatest weapon is the churches voice or language: when we leave Red Oak Grove wherever we go we should all be saying the same thing about the church and The Lord.

We should be saying we love The Lord at Red Oak:

We love each other at Red Oak:

We love what The Lord is doing with our ministry at Red Oak:

Then other people will hear the same message from everybody. They will want to come and be a part of a church that loves The Lord and is on one accord with one language. Touch your neighbor and help me preach tell them to learn our language if they don't know our language.

Our language is centered around the love of God, the grace of God, the compassion of God, and the favor of God. In other words, God has been good to us and its only because we speak the same language. Not only does this text say that The Lord said the people are one and not only does The Lord say the people are speaking one language. But The Lord said this is only the beginning of what they will be able to do.

You have to get this in your spirit. Red Oak has come this far be faith and accomplished all that it has but this is only the beginning of what we can do. If the church by faith has done as much as it has think of the possibility of what the church can do in the future. Unity put us in a position to achieve goals that we don't even realize are possible.

The tower and the city were only a fraction of what the

people would have been able to do. As a matter of fact, the conclusion of verse six says nothing that they propose to do will now be impossible for them.

Can you imagine a church with the resources of unlimited possibility with the help of The Lord? Can you see every member of Red Oak Grove working together to do God's will as purposed by God? Before something becomes a reality, you have to see it in your mind. In other words, for success to become a part of your fabric you first have to see yourself as successful. I see more ministries because of the unity of God; I see more people coming ad joining because of the unity of God. I see more children being blessed because of the unity of God at this church.

I see the church that reflects the Glory of God, and nothing that the church purpose to do will now be impossible to do because the church is going to get on one accord. The old hymn writer had it right when these words were pinned When all God's children get together what a time, what a time. The church is going to march together to the one drumbeat. The church is going to have the same sound from everybody. The sound of praise and giving God glory. The church is going to be one and God is going to be the center of it all.

The world needs a unified church

The community needs a unified church

Our children need a unified church.

The church needs the unity, to do Gods will.

Walk together children don't get weary, there's a great camp meeting in the promised land, we are going walk and never get tired.

Dr. J. A. Gladney

Together We Can

Red Oak Grove
October 13, 2019
Pericope: Matthew 12: 22-32
Subject: Together We Can
Behavioral purpose: To move hearers to get on one accord
Rev. Dr. J. A. Gladney

Some missionaries in the Philippines set up a croquet game in their front yard. Several of their native neighbors became interested and wanted to join the fun. The missionaries explained the game and started them out, each with a mallet and ball. As the game progressed, opportunity came for one of the players to take advantage of another by knocking that person's ball out of the court.

A missionary explained the procedure, but his advice only puzzled the Native friend. "Why would I want to knock his ball out of the court?" he asked. "So you will be the one to win!" a missionary said. The short-statured man, clad only in a loincloth, shook his head in bewilderment. Competition is generally ruled out in a hunting and gathering society, where people survive not by competing but by sharing equally in every activity.

The game continued, but no one followed the missionaries 'advice. When a player successfully got through all the wickets, the game was not over for him. He went back and gave aid and advice to his fellows. As the final player moved toward the last wicket, the affair was still very much a team effort. And finally, when the last wicket was played, the "team" shouted happily, "We won! We won!"

That is how the Church, the body of Christ, should be. We're a team. **We all win together...**

You have heard all of your life there is no I in team. When one of us succeed we all succeeded. When one of us fail we all fail. We are in this together, collectively, working in collaboration, jointly, in unity. Unity is God's work to make the world into a home. Psalms 133:1 Behold, how good and how pleasant it is for brethren to dwell together in unity!

Ecclesiastes 4:9 Two are better than one, Because they have a good reward for their labor.
Ecclesiastes 4:10 For if they fall, one will lift up his companion. But woe to him who is alone when he falls, for he has no one to help him up.
Ecclesiastes 4:11 Again, if two lie down together, they will keep warm; But how can one be warm alone?
Ecclesiastes 4:12. Though one may be overpowered by another, two can withstand him. And a threefold cord is not quickly broken.
We will never become a church that effectively reaches out to those who are missing out if we shoot our wounded and major on the minuses. Instead of being fishers of men, as Christ has called us, we will be keepers of an ever-shrinking aquarium. This fall when you see geese heading south for the winter, flying along in V formation, you might be interested in knowing what science has discovered about why they fly that way. It has been learned that as each bird flaps its wings, it creates uplift for the bird immediately following. By flying in a V formation, the whole flock adds at least 71 percent greater flying range than if each bird flew on its own.

In other words, if the geese fly together, they can cover more ground and they want to work as hard. (Christians who share a common direction, and a sense of community can get where they are going quicker and easier, because they are traveling on the thrust of one another.) We like geese can get more done if we stay together and work together. Whenever a goose falls out of formation, it suddenly feels the drag and resistance of trying to go at it alone, and quickly gets back into formation to take advantage of the lifting power of the bird immediately in front.

(If we have as much sense as a goose, we will stay in formation with those who are headed the same way we are going.)

The goal of every church should be to win more souls for Christ and have a greater impact on the community. If we have the same goal and are headed in the same direction, then there is no need of one person trying to do the work of 600 hundred people. When the lead goose gets tired, he rotates back in the wing and another goose flies point. Geese know that if they are going to be successful that they have to rotate leadership. Geese know that if the one out front gets tried, weary, burnout, and frustrated all they have to do is fall back and let another goose that is fresh and ready take the lead. The goose that takes the lead is chosen because that goose can handle turbulence. Every goose can't handle turbulence because the lead goose takes on the most wind in the formation. (It pays to take turns doing hard jobs—with people at church or with geese flying south.)

Not only do they rotate leadership, but they also give affirmation to the one leading. The geese honk from behind to encourage those up front to keep up their speed. The led goose know that he is not out there by himself because behind him is a pack of geese honking letting him know I got your back.

What if at home the momma honk for dad while he working instead of fussing? What if daddy honk for momma while she is doing her thank instead of complaining? What is momma and daddy honk for the children as they learn and develop? What would the church be like if we like goose honk for each other to help each other be your best self you can be so we could in turn get more done?

What if when the lead singer is singing in choir the background is clapping and waiting for their part and not pouting because they are not leading? What if when the ushers are working and worshipping the pew is appreciative for their service and acts of kindness rather than being mean to them and rude. What if when the deacon is praying and reading the scripture those in background are honking with amen and praise the lord rather than being cool, calm, and collective, with your arms folded, and your mouth closed?

What if when the Pastor is preaching and the word is going fourth the congregation is honking: preach preacher, go head, rather than looking like you drank sour lemon juice for breakfast, and ate prunes for dinner? The geese in back honk for the ones out front. Can we pause and honk for Jesus and tell Him thank you for another day? Can we let the Lord know we got each other's back?

Not only do geese rotate leadership, not only do they cheer for each other, but they take care of each other.

Finally, when a goose gets sick, or is wounded by a shot and falls out, two geese fall out of formation and follow him down to help and protect him. They stay with him until he is either able to fly, or until he is dead, and then they launch out on their own or with another formation to catch up with their original group. (If people knew we would stand by them like that in church, they would push down these walls to get in.)

You see, all we have to do in order to attract those who are missing back to church is to demonstrate to the world that we have as much sense as geese here at church. The greatness of a church is not measured in how many come into the church but in how many go out in ministry. Matthew 28:19 Go therefore and make disciples of all the nations, baptizing them in the name of the Father and of the Son and of the Holy Spirit. The church gathers, then the church scatters.

The church must go outside its walls to reach people who need the Lord. The effectiveness of our church is shown in the work that is done together as the body of Christ. In our text of attention, we see a man that has two problems that those who bring him to Jesus wants Jesus to address the man is **blind** and **unable to speak**. This man is both death and dumb. But his condition is not the result of what he has but what has him. He is possessed by a devil.

Some people problem is not what they have but what has them. When a person is demon possessed, they are controlled by what is on the inside of them. This man's problem was that he was possessed by a demon and not a devil. There is only one devil but multitudes of demons. Have you ever said of someone I don't know what is wrong with you, medicine can't solve what you have, the doctors can't figure out what the problem is? Maybe just maybe the problem is a misdiagnosis of the current situation. You have been trying to deal with that person on the devil level and they are demon possessed.

It's not one thing that's the problem they are dealing with

a multitude of things going on. Have you ever come across someone who if they can't run it, they will tear it all up? If it is not their way, it's the highway. Maybe that person or those persons have been misdiagnosed maybe we are not dealing with a devil, but we are dealing demon possession. The Bible describes the action of a devil this way. John 10:10 The thief does not come except to steal, and to kill, and to destroy.

If someone Is stealing the peace in the church and destroying the unity and fellowship of the church and killing those that seek peace and want to destroy things, then those are characteristics of the devil. Jesus says I have come that they may have life, and that they may have it more abundantly. Demon possession was not an ordinary physical disease. In other words, you can't cure it with an aspirin, or flu shot.

This demoniac's condition was not due to functional or organic disorder, so Jesus dealt not with the apparent malady but its root or cause by casting out the demon. Does anybody have anything going on in your life that needs not rebuking but casting out? Some stuff needs to cast out in the name of Jesus.......

Cast of fear

cast out doubt

Cast out depression

Cast out bulling

Cast out a spirit that want follow leadership....

Some stuff has to be cut off from its roots and dealt with

head on. You know wrong is just wrong and right is right. 1 Corinthians 14:40 Let all things be done decently and in order. We don't know if Jesus laid his hands on the man, we don't know if he spoke and the man was healed, we don't know what actions Jesus took in the text all we know is that the Bible says He-Jesus healed him, and when he healed him, he could both speak and see. The man could speak correctly and see clearly because he was restored to sanity rather than a bodily imperfection removed.

When demons are cast out the vision of the church can be seen clearly, and mission followed correctly. Notice two things happened when the miracle occurred. One group was happy. The other group was mad. It's interesting that two groups of people can see the same thing and leave feeling different about it. **What impress those that are for Jesus angers those that are against Jesus.** When miracles happen and blessing fall it ought to impress followers of Jesus. When the church is growing, and the spirit is high it ought to impress flowers of Jesus.

When good things are happening in your life it ought to impress followers of Jesus. When God is blessing, and your life is in order it ought to impress followers of Jesus. One group said he must be the Son of David. The other group said he cats out demon only by Beelzebub which was the prince of demons. Here is the problem with the text. They the Pharisees were supposed to be the leaders and they were the ones who kept the law, the people looked to them to do what Jesus was doing.

People would come to them with their problems and issues, and they would help solve them. They could deal with some stuff, but a deaf and dumb demon possessed man was out of there reach and Jesus comes along and is able to do what they can't do, so instead of praising God they talk down about the miracle. Jesus dealt with their thoughts and the things they were thinking.

Proverbs 23:7 says For as he thinks in his heart, so is he.

Luke 6:45 says A good man out of the good treasure of his heart brings forth good; and an evil man out of the evil treasure of his heart brings forth evil. For out of the abundance of the heart his mouth speaks. Matthew 12:34 says Brood of vipers! How can you, being evil, speak good things? For out of the abundance of the heart the mouth speaks.

Jesus dealt with their thoughts because thoughts lead to action. Notice what Jesus said Matthew 12:25 "Every kingdom divided against itself is brought to desolation, and every city or house divided against itself will not stand. The saying about the kingdom divided teaches a basic lesson of political science **in unity there is strength.** If the church is not unified it can't do greater works for the kingdom of God.

There are a hurting people in our community, but a divided house can't help addressing their needs. There are failing schools in the black community, but a divided house can't help educating our children. There are political and economic issues that grip our communities, but a divided house can't help addressing the needs of the larger society. There are families that are being torn apart right under our noises, but a divided house can't help addressing the needs of a family in crises.

Isn't That Good News

January 13, 2019
Second Sunday of the Year
Text: Ephesians 4:3-6
Pericope: Ephesians 4: 1-13
Subject: Isn't That Good News (What if, why not, Unity)
Behavioral Purpose: To move hearers to become more unified in all of their efforts so the kingdom of God can be furthered.

Last Sunday we talked about these two words in dept: What If and Why Not? Then we concluded that sermon with moving from making this the year of some more and not the year of no more. On this second Sunday in this new year, we are going to continue the theme of What If Why Not and add to that the word Unity. What If Why Not Unity in 2019. Tonto and the Lone Ranger were riding through a canyon together when all of a sudden both sides were filled with Native American warriors on horses, dressed for battle.

The Lone Ranger turned to Tonto and asked, *"**What are we going to do?**"* Tonto replied, "What you mean 'we, ' Whiteman?" That's the way some in the church think, but it ought never be that way. We are in this thing together, we are stronger together, together we stand divided we fall, and all we have is the Lord and one another.

There must be love.
There must be peace.
There must be unity!

In The fourth chapter of Ephesians. I want to remind you that Paul is writing about the theme of unity in the church. Specifically, Paul has been teaching us how to Maintain the Unity of The Church. Achieving unity within a group can sometimes be a difficult endeavor. Only because we come from so many different backgrounds. We have differing ideas about many different subjects. We were all raised different. We possess differing goals, ambitions, and agendas in life.

If we are honest with ourselves and each other, we will admit that Unity in an atmosphere can be hard to come by. I would say that unity in the church would be an absolute impossibility if it were solely up to us. Thank God it is not up to us alone.

We play a great part in the unity of the church, as we see in **verses 1-3**. However, *The Place of Our Unity* in the church is not in our ability to produce it all by ourselves. The unity of the church, like everything else we have as the people of God, rests on His grace alone. Walking in unity does not mean that we always have the same ideas about the same issues. We may have differences of opinion from time to time. That is both healthy and good. There needs to be a diversity of thought and not an intellectual or spiritual totalitarianism that dictates what every single person is allowed to think and believe.

Walking in unity does not means that we will always believe exactly the same about every single issue where doctrine is concerned. It does not mean that we lose our individualism when we are saved. It does mean that we are marked by a common purpose and led by a common Savior. It does mean that when the Lord gives us His clear direction, we put aside our personal opinions and walk together for the glory of God and the good of the Gospel. It does mean that the unity of the church is more important than me getting my way, or you are getting yours. It does mean that the unity of the church always comes ahead of my personal agenda.

It does mean that the unity of the church comes before

my feelings. While we the people are the church, we the people are also the problem. We, the people who make up the local church, are the guardians of the unity produced within us by the Holy Spirit, but we are also the greatest danger to that unity. Why is that?

Many reasons could be listed, but I will mention just a few for the sake of time.

- We are all sinners who possess a fallen nature. Some people motto is y'all have sinned but in reality, it's all have sinned.... that mindset destroys unity....

- We are sometimes selfish, self-centered, and want our own way. That mindset destroys unity

- We are jealous when we see others succeed, get blessed or be promoted.

- We get angry when we think we have been wronged.

- We act out of spite hoping to hurt those we think have hurt us.

- We fail to forgive the wrongs done to us by other.

- We fail to love the Lord like we should, thus we cannot love others like we should.

- By the way, when you fail to give love, you are not in a position to receive love either!

- We allow our sinful natures to be manifested in all our human interactions.

- We are brought together from different backgrounds,

with different views about right and wrong, and with different opinions about how things ought to be done.

- We have different agendas in life. That is, we have different opinions about what the church should be, should do, and how it should operate.

Paul has been teaching us in Ephesians that God, by His grace, and through the Gospel of Jesus Christ, has brought together people from every imaginable background, and has made them one in Jesus Christ. Jews who were born under the Law and who are subject to the Law, and Gentiles who were given over to dumb idols, have been brought together in one body. The ground of our unity does not rest in our ability to get along with one another. Our unity in the body of Christ rests upon the common *éléments* that we share as members of His body.

All of the *éléments* Paul mentions in these verses are freely given to us by the grace of God. They are the fruit of our relationship with Him. It is these *éléments* that make unity within the church a real possibility. Paul mentions seven common *éléments* that all believers share in Christ. He groups these *éléments* into three *areas*. These *areas* serve to teach us that unity in the church comes from our relationship with the Godhead. Every member of the trinity is involved making unity possible within the church. Let's examine these *areas* and the *éléments* together today as we consider **The Place of Our Unity**.

Building Up the Church

Church Anniversary 13 years
Second Sunday in March
Text: Ephesians 4:11-15
Pericope: Ephesians 4: 1-16
Subject Building Up the Church
Behavioral Purpose: To move hearers to hold it together and stay together, and work to build up the church!
Start of my fourth year after 3rd year anniversary
Rev. Dr. J. A. Gladney

Every now and then we need to do an assessment to see how we are doing; in other words, we need to ask critical and yet challenging questions to see if we have made little or any progress. Part of our mission is to involve every member in ministry.

The critical question is, how are we doing so far with involving the members of Red Oak in the work of the ministry of Red Oak that is a good question to head us in the right direction on year three?

Help me do a quick assessment look down your row to your left and to your right, turn around and look behind you. Now do you see someone who is a ***member*** and not a ***visitor*** who is not involved in ministry.

If so, what are you going to do about it?

Are you going to go to them and invite them to be a part of the church body or are you just going to let them walk in and out of Red Oak without doing their part? Red Oak is a lot of things but one thing it is not is a **Mortuary**-where corpse's walk in and walk out, dead in their sin and "trespasses." Red Oak is not a ***vacation spot*** where people only come once or twice a year. It most certainly is not a ***Convalescent home*** where people just sit around and wait to die. It most certainly is not an ***Icehouse***, where people with, Cold hearts give others the cold shoulder"

If you notice with eyes of expectancy, you will find a text that full and pregnant with preaching possibility. Notice in verse 11 All Christians are to be equipped for the work of active spiritual service. After the Christological interpretation of the scripture citation translated after you understand who Jesus Christ is or you have some understanding of Christ for yourself then you can go deeper in the work of the church.

You can't live your whole life off of what somebody else said about Jesus. At some point you have got to get to know Jesus for yourself. My testimony is Jesus is my way out of no way that means to me personally when I couldn't find my way Jesus showed me the way. He guided me to safety while in my personal storm. Jesus is my bridge over trouble waters that means Jesus allowed some stuff to pass under and over me he hid me and guided me to safety.

After you understand who Jesus is then you have to develop a theology of the ecclesiological, everyone says ***ecclesiological*** which is an understanding of the church. In other words, if you love the church and are a part of the church you will not just sit there you will get up and do something.

The Missionary Ministry meets every third Monday join them and help them do something, they put food in the emergency room at the hospital, the give food to Sanctuary Hospice House, the clean the Health Clinic, they are involved on our district, state, and local level, don't just sit there do something.

Our brotherhood meets every third Sunday morning if

you are a man, and you are not involved don't just sit there do something. The newly media ministry needs bright dedicated minds with a thirst for technology and theology, don't just sit there do something. There are several ministries we don't have, if we don't have a ministry in your area of passion we will start it today, don't just sit there do something.

Our Sunday School ministry have classes for all ages come and learn something. We need to have an average of 100 people in Sunday School every Sunday, and the reason why we don't is because you want to come. Help me preach. Tell your neighbor, "He talking about you!" Our Bible study class on Wednesday night has classes for all ages-come and learn something. The Third Grade Stop Gate test requires that you do something. Mrs. Cason, Mrs. King, Mrs. Metcalf, Mrs. Marshall, need more people to come and visit them, sit with them, and talk with them, they are demanding that you do something.

Consider this illustration from A little boy was overheard talking to himself as he strode through his backyard, baseball, cap in place and toting ball and bat. "I'm the greatest baseball player in the world, "he said proudly. Then he tossed the ball in the air, swung, and missed. Undaunted, he picked up the ball, threw it into the air and said to himself, I'm the greatest player ever!" He swung at the ball again, and again he missed.

He paused a moment to examine the bat and ball carefully. Then once again he threw the ball into the air and said, I'm the greatest baseball player who ever lived." He swung the bat hard, and again missed the ball. Wow! he exclaimed "What a pitcher!" Come here lean in don't let what you are not good at stop you from what you are great at.

Verse 12 uses the word edify: everybody shout edify. It's a short word with an important meaning. To edify is to build up. The goal in this text is to build up the body of Christ or the church.

What can we do to build up our church? I'm glad you asked, I'm also glad you are following along.

The first thing this pericope suggest we can do to build up the church is to **_Put Away Our Differences_**! It's in verse 13 Till we all come in the unity of the faith. Unity is vital for a church to be effective. If the church needs anything it needs everyone to be on one accord. You remember the famous line from Drum Line- One Band One Sound-we are one church with one sound. As a matter of fact, Ephesians 4:4-5 says, "There is one body and one Spirit — just as you were called to one hope at your calling — one Lord, one faith, one baptism,"

The culture of a church changes when we all get together and get on the same page. Those in the upper room were of one accord (Acts 1:14) On the day of Pentecost all were of one accord (Acts 2:1) Can I let you in on a secret and that secret is Power flows through a united church. Love flows through a united church. Joy flows through a united church. Worship that is meaningful flows through a united church. Ministry that is real flows through a united church. Chains are broken, souls are saved, and lives are transformed when the church is united.

The preaching is more powerful, praying is more uplifting, singing is more anointed, usher stand taller, when the church is united.   Not only does this pericope suggest we can put away our differences in order to build up the church, but it also points to the fact that we can build up the church ***by focusing on Jesus***.

It's in the "C" clause of verse 13 if you don't know what the c clause is that means you need to be in Bible study. It's says to the measure of the stature of the fullness of Christ. People may fail us, but Jesus never fails. The secret to consistent Christian Living is Jesus. In John 16:33 he said be of good cheer; I have overcome the world. In Revelation 1:11 he said "I am alpha and Omega, the first and the last. In John 11:25 Jesus said unto her, I am the resurrection and life; he that believeth in me, though he were dead, yet shall he live. I would like to suggest three life changing word that are found in Hebrews 12:2 those words are ***Looking unto Jesus***'

These words eliminate all excuses for failure

    They erase all past mistake

    They give hope and possibility to the lost

    These words help strengthen the weak

    They help lift the downtrodden

Yes, the words Looking unto Jesus

    Points to Heavens salvation for earth damnation

    Heavens blessing for earth's curse

    Heavens' response for earth's revenge

    Heaven's glory for earth's gloom

Heaven's solution for earth's problems.

When you were in trouble have you ever found those words to be a comfort to you: Looking unto Jesus. Has anybody ever had to look unto Jesus, or call on Jesus? When you called on Jesus didn't The Lord come and see about you. You are still here only because Jesus allowed it, Jesus kept you. This pericope also suggests that we not only Focus on Jesus, but it also give birth to the fact that we can build up the church by **_Getting back to the basics_**. It's pointed out in verse 14.

Many times, the flaunted efforts to build up churches flounder because the emphasis may be on programs rather than on people. Part of our vision says we should strive to as a church to become people friendly. People don't want to know how much we got going on until they know that we are genuinely concerned about them and their personally welfare. Other times the church effort fail to build up the church is because churches sometimes search for strategy rather than saving sinners. If Red Oak Grove is going to be successful and relevant, we must build on sound doctrine, not supposed new revelations.

Ephesians 4:14 says "That we henceforth be no more children, tossed to and fro, and carried about with every wind of doctrine, by the sleight of men, and cunning craftiness, whereby they lie in wait to deceive;" The Bible should take priority over everything! Take 10 minutes day to read your Bible, take 10 minutes a day to pray and take 10 minutes a day to exercise. Training up are children in the way they should go should remain a priority. Making sure we focus on build strong marriages up should remain a propriety. If divorce is going to be stopped it starts with the church and the bible. Making sure we allow our Senior Citizens the room and support to lead the church from a foundational standpoint of view should remain a priority.

But most importantly saving souls should also be the churches focus. How many of you know that the winds of false doctrine are ever blowing? The winds of itching ears are blowing. People wanting to hear only what they think is profitable. Cunning counterfeit characters are waiting to deceive the church. Cunning counterfeit shade throwers are lurking around the church.

Dr. J. A. Gladney

Biblical Leadership, Unity, and team Building

Red Oak Grove
Pericope: Ephesians 4:1-5
Subject: Biblical Leadership, Unity, and team Building
Behavioral Purpose: To Move here's to come together and to also change positions
Rev. Dr. Jeffery A. Gladney

Red Oak Grove is a great church, I think you can agree with me when I say that, but it can become an even greater church. I told them on Last Wednesday night that there is another level you can go to we should never become satisfied with good when greater is possible. Leaders make the difference, and training makes the difference in the leaders. All leaders are born, but they are not born leaders.

A leader must earn a following. You have heard the saying people don't care how much you know until the know how much you care. But what is given or attained in an access to a leadership position is no more than an opportunity for one to become the leader for which the position calls. A church needs leaders and leadership. It deserves and requires both. God has promised His church His presence and His leadership, along with His power and other resources. Among the resources He has given are people to lead.

Tell your neighbor you are one of God best gifts to the church that you are a member of....

The members of the church are God's gifts to churches; and the individual gifts they have been given comes with the gift of themselves. I hold heartily believe that God has given Red Oak everything and everybody it needs to be a successful church for many generations to come. It is true that just because you hold a position that does not make you a leader. A leader is one who has followers. It has been described this way that real leadership is influence. **No followers-no leader.** If you are leading and no one is following you then you are just out taking a stroll.

Leadership is what one does to get followers. However good leadership is not just getting people to follow you because you can be dead wrong and those who are following you, want to go along to get along, then those following you will end up in a ditch with you. This is how the Bible says it Matthew 15:14 Let them alone. They are blind leaders of the blind. And if the blind leads the blind, both will fall into a ditch."

Good leadership is working appropriately with other leaders and followers to determine outcomes that are desired and right and to progress cooperatively and effectively toward their realization. Paul gives us an example of leadership, unity, and team building in the 4th chapter of Ephesians. The apostle Paul labored to foster unity amidst a diverse population-in other words, he worked at team building. If we are going to be successful, we are going to have to work together. When we work together, we display a servant's attitude toward leadership.

We can do more together than we can apart: We can help more people when we work together. We can build up our communities when we work together. I believe it was Rodney King who said Why Can't We All Just Get along. Can I pull over long enough to tell someone that a leader is nothing more than a servant. There is always room at the top for anyone who is willing to say, "I'll serve." True Christian Leadership always begins with servanthood.

Selfishness always ends in self-destruction. John Ruskin said, "When a person is wrapped up in themselves, he makes a pretty small package." There are several words in the Greek language for servant, and Paul used one that best conveyed the idea of a lowly servant. The Greek word here is hupertes which means an under rower. In those days, large wooden tiered ships called trireme. These large ships were propelled by slaves chained to their oars in the hull of the ship. These slaves on the lowest tier were called under rowers. In order for the ship to move the under rower had to row in the same direction at the same time.

Paul and his co-workers didn't want to be exalted; they wanted to be known as third-level galley slaves who pulled oars. Are there any under rowers in Red Oak. Are there any people who can say if I have to play second fiddle just let me do my part? Many people want to serve unless they are the leader but what about serving from the background. What about serving if your name if not called? What about serving if you don't get a pat on the back beloved God wants obedient servants. 1 Corinthians 4:2 Paul says, "it is required in stewards, that a man be found faithful."

God does not want a person to come up with a clever new way to pull his oar and shear off everyone else's in the process! He wants faithful rowers who see themselves as willing servants. Paul here in Ephesians reminds them of the attitude of the individual players. (4:1-3) Then he discusses the attitude of the corporate body (3:4-6) Paul insists there is a sevenfold oneness: he says there is one body, one Spirt, One Hope, One Lord, One faith, One baptism, and One God and Father.

Notice First for preaching purposes these attitudes that leader should possess and every member of the church for that matter.

The pivotal verse of the whole letter may be this first verse. It gathers up a single phrase (the vocation wherewith ye are called) the theme of chapters 1-3, and in a very straight forward appeal to leaders walk worthy this verse announces the emphasis of chapters 4-6. The inference is that the high calling the Christian has experienced carries with it very weighty responsibilities. One of those great and weighty responsibilities is that Leaders and Christian walk-in unity.

When a leader works with the Pastor they are walking in unity, notice you don't have to like the Person-but you should respect the office of Pastor. When a leader shows ready to serve regularly then the leader is walking in unity. When a leader is systematic giver or tither then they are walking in unity. When a leader supports every ministry of the church then they are walking in unity. Walk a word characteristic of the last half of Ephesians (4:1, 17, 5:2 8, 15) Walk is used in the scripture to define the course of one's life. Your walk is your personal lifestyle.

In Genesis, for example Enoch is said to have walked with God. And John reminds us of our obligation as Christians to walk even as Jesus waked (1 John 2:6) To walk worthy of the vocation wherewith ye are called means to live in a way that is in harmony with our vocation. That word vocation speaks of the calling, or the invitation that belongs to every leader and every Christian.

It's a blessing to be able to serve.

It's a blessing to make a joyful noise unto the Lord

It's a blessing to be able to lead others to higher heights and deeper depths in the Lord.

The Calling or gift of leadership is a precious privilege. It is a divine blessing.

This text has given birth to the attitudes that leaders should have but it also shed light on the Character of the leader.

The understanding of character is that it describes a person's attributes. Character is what you do when no one is watching. In other words, you character describes a person at their core. Character speaks of the foundational principle by which a person lives out their lives. The following verse of this passage gives some practical details about how the Christian is to walk worthy of the calling. What does walking worthy look like? How can walking worthy be recognized? Verse 2 lists five Spiritual qualities that characterize the Christian who walk worthy of his/her leadership calling.

Lowliness- speaks of humility, if you are leader and you are humble it will take you a long way. The Modern song says sit down and be humble!

be humble when you serve

be humble when you lead

be humble in all you undertake to do

Notice being High-mindedness leads to division and breakup. Meekness-conveys the notion of gentleness toward people and submission to God. Just because a leader or person is meek does not mean that they are weak. If you are a meek leader, you are mild, patient, and restrained. Long suffering- is the opposite of short-temperedness. Long suffering has the idea of a leader that is slow to anger. You can't be a leader and every time someone rub you the wrong way you are ready to roll your neck, snap your fingers and set it off.

Forbearance is the fourth quality that attends the worthy leader or Christian life. If you are forbearing, you are able to make allowance for the faults of fellow believers. This also means you are willing to bear with them in weakness and failings. Forbearance means being able to put up with a lot. I don't quit because things are not going my way when I am forbearing. I don't jump ship because I have to change positions or let someone else row. I don't take my Bible put it under my arm and leave when I am forbearing. Lastly this verse says bearing with one another in Love.

In Love shows that my role in leadership was done with the right frame of heart. In Love shows that I did not serve grudgingly or because no one else would serve. I serve because I Love the Lord. The Greek word suggest the attitude that seeks the highest good of others, Love Covers A multitude of faults.

Now Is the Time for Unity

Preached June 29, 2015
Red Oak Grove
Pericope: 1 Corinthians 1:1-10
Text: 1 Corinthians 1:10
Subject: Now Is the Time for Unity
Behavioral Purpose: To move hearers to join God in his redemptive work for unity
Dr. J. A. Gladney

Last Sunday we started talking about a new theme that we will focus on for the remainder of this year: and that theme is together we can. In that sermonic discourse we highlighted the fact that we are better toastier and together we can get more done.

Unity is like learning to play on a team together. "At one point during a game, the coach said to one of his young players, "Do you understand what cooperation is? What a team is?"

The little boy nodded in the affirmative. "Do you understand that what matters is whether we win together as a team." The little boy nodded yes. "So," the coach continued, "When a strike is called, or you're out at first, you don't argue or curse or attack the umpire. Do you understand all that?" Again, the little boy nodded. "Good," said the coach. "Now go over there and explain it to your father."

As the human founder of the Corinthian church, Paul had a really big task before him. Paul loved his Corinthian brothers and sisters in Christ. But when he received reports that divisions, immorality, and pride had crept their way into the church, he knew he had to speak up and confront the sin that some members of the church had grown proud of.

Paul uses the "sandwich approach" to deal with problems. To use this approach, begin with a compliment, address the problem, and then end with another compliment. In the first nine verses of this chapter, Paul began with a compliment, but now starting in verse 10, he begins to address one of the problems in the church-**divisions**. Paul knows this problem must be solved. If we were to be honest with ourselves, we know that like Paul we can't allow sin to go unchallenged in the church.

It should forever be the position of the church that wrong is wrong, and sin is sin no matter how you try to explain the sin, or congress legislate the law, you can't legislate morality and all sin is wrong.

According to our Bible study lesson Journeying into Biblical problem solving in verses 1-3 we see in the greeting Sanctification, 1 Corinthians 1:2 <u>Unto the church of God, which is at Corinth, to them that are sanctified in Christ Jesus, called to be saints, with all that in every place call upon the name of Jesus Christ our Lord, both theirs and ours:</u>

To be sanctified means to be set apart from sin for God's use.

I might as well pull over long enough to tell you that if you are saved you have been set apart, if you have been set apart, you are sanctified not for your own will, but to do the will of God. Sanctification is not just for the sanctified church it's for all Christians that are trying to live right, do right, and be right. In verses 4-6 of our text of attention we see **transformation**, Paul says I thank my God always on your behalf why because of the grace of God which is given to you by Christ Jesus. (4) Paul reminds them that because of the grace of Christ Jesus they are blessed.

It's not only the church of Corinth that is blessed because of God's grace but we are blessed because of His grace in our lives. You do know what grace is don't you? Grace has been described as God's Riches at Christ Expense. You do know that you have been kept not because you have been so holy, and lived so upright, and said all the right things but you are blessed because of grace. All of our blessings are completely undeserved, but because of His grace, God blesses us anyway.

Grace woke you up when death tried to keep you sleep this morning. Grace kept you in your right mind when everyone around you was losing their mind. Grace gives you the strength to press on in-spite of the cares of this world and the weight they place on us. I don't know about you, but I thank God for his grace. Grace that can lift us from the gutters to unto glory from prison unto paradise from hell unto heaven from despair to delight from shadows unto sunshine and from emptiness to everything. If we keep reading in verses 7-9, we see **participation**. Leadership rule # 1 is this: affirmation comes before confrontation. Although Corinth had some ***problem people***, Paul still saw the good in them. No matter how bad you think someone is or maybe you should always find something good in them.

Just for the sake of preaching allow me to say that there is no such thing as a perfect church, if you just so happen to find such a church don't join it or it want to be perfect anymore. Paul starts our verse of attention off by begging them in the words of "Now I beseech you brethren. (Verse 10) Paul does not come to them in the power of his own name or his own strength, but Paul comes to them in the name of Jesus. There is no saving grace in the name of Gladney, but at the name of

Jesus every knee must bow, and every tongue confess that Jesus Christ is Lord.

Notice the placement of Paul's words: Now I beseech you, brethren, by the name of our Lord Jesus Christ. When Paul called Him Lord-Paul was recognizing His authority as a teacher or rabbi. You do know that Lord is a title not his name. Lord is a title of dignity and honor acknowledging the power and authority of the one addressed. When we call Jesus Lord, we are recognizing that he has dignity and honor and power because of his authority. Jesus does not require any other authority's permission, because He is The Authority.

He needs no other superior's concession because He is The Superior. He demands no other master's sanction because He is The Master.

We see that Paul not only address Him with authority, but Paul also calls Him Jesus. For Etymology purposes you do know that Jesus is his name. Jesus is derived from a Hebrew word that means "savior." Jesus demonstrated time and time again that he came to save mankind from their sin.

Jesus came down through 42 generations, left the royal streets of glory to be wrapped in swaddling clothes and laid in a manger, Jesus healed the sick, Jesus gave sight to the blind, unstopped deaf ears, and made the lame to walk and the dumb to talk. Jesus died at a place called Calvary for the sins of the whole world.

If anything in this life should give you hope it is the fact that you have been set free from the trap of sin that you were in. Christ is Jesus's title which means anointed and refers to one commissioned by God for a special task. Paul lets the reader know he has a clear Christological understanding of who Jesus is. If you are going to be a better Christian, you have to know who Jesus is for yourself. Your whole life can't be lived off of someone else's understating of Jesus at some point you have got to get to know him for yourself.

Paul understood that the focus should always remain on the one that has authority to save us because of the commission he has been given by God. There are three things that this text highlights for preaching clarification that arrest our attention. Can I show them to you and go to my seat?

The first thing that arrested me in this text was a clear proclamation. Notice it for yourself that you all speak the same thing. I have used this illustration before you remember the movie drum line-in that movie the bands' theme was we are one band with one sound. That holds true for Red Oak we are one church with one sound. Help Me preach let's say that together: We are One Church with One Sound. That is the sound of love. That is the sound of following the leadership of the church. That is the sound keeping God at the center of all we do. That is the sound of helping more people, saving more souls.

That is the sound of walking together, working together, and staying together. The pastor should not be saying one thing and a small group in the church saying something else. One Sunday school lesson some time ago put it this way: we don't want to become a bowl of spoiling fruit, detached from Our God who gives life, slowly rotting even as we appear shiny and delicious. No Paul tells the church at Corinth, the church he founded, that they should all be saying the same thing.

If we believe that Red Oak is a great church there should be no and if's or but about it, we should all be saying the same thing. If we believe that can't no body do me like Jesus, we should all be saying the same thing. If We believe that Jesus is the best thing that ever happened to me, then we should all be saying the same thing. Come on let's practice all saying the same thing! Shout! Thank You Jesus!

Not only do I see clear proclamation in this text, but I also see in the text a Clear Demonstration. And that there be no divisions among you. In mathematics division is splitting up into groups or parts. Paul was in essence saying that there be no small factions among you, that there be no splitting up into cliques, that there be no big I's and little U's. The Bible is clear on what it says about division. John 17:21 says "That they all may be one; as thou, Father, art in me, and I in thee, that they also may be one in us: that the world may believe that thou hast sent me." Psalms 133:1 says "Behold, how good and how pleasant it is for brethren to dwell together in unity!" 1 Corinthians 3:3 says "For ye are yet carnal: for whereas there is among you envying, and strife, and divisions, are ye not carnal, and walk as men?"

Anything with two heads is a monster. There is only one vision there cannot be two visions in one church or division. Habakkuk 2:2 "And the Lord answered me and said. Write **the** vision and make it plain upon tables. That he may run that readeth it." Unity matter because division exposes us as carnal. Ephesians 4:5 says, "One Lord, one faith, one baptism," Unity matters because division destroys our witness. This text has given birth to the fact that we have a clear proclamation, and it has given birth to the fact that we should make a clear demonstration.

Lastly it lifts for sermonic purposes that we set forth a **clear presentation.** In the words: But is a conjunction. When you break this verse down it is saying but being a together church is better than being a divided church. Mark 3:25 says "And if a house be divided against itself, that house cannot stand." Being a together family is much better than being a divided family. But when preachers and deacons are together it's much better than preachers and deacons being divided. But when the choir and congregation is together, it's much better than the choir and congregation being divided. But when the ushers and greeters are together it's much better than the ushers and greets being divided. But when the children, youth, young adults, Senior Citizens, are together its, much better than the children, youth, young adults, and Senior Citizens being divided.

When we are together its much, much better than us being divided. But that ye be perfectly joined together in the same mind and in the same judgement. You have heard the old saying before together we stand divided, we fall. Notice that falling for the church is not an option because. If we fall there will be no future Red Oak, because our children will fall with us. If we fall the community around us will fall, because it still takes a village to raise a child. I don't know about you but for me falling is not an option, being divided is not a choice.

Dr. J. A. Gladney

Questions for Sermons

This form is intended to inform and assist in gathering needed information. Your honesty is appreciated. Please answer the following in complete sentences:

Name_____

Date_____

Title of Sermon_____

Scripture Reference for Sermon_____

1. Did this sermon impact your thinking about unity in a negative or positive way? Explain.

   _____
   _____
   _____
   _____
   _____

2. Has your understanding of unity changed since hearing this sermon?

   _____
   _____
   _____
   _____
   _____

3. What areas about unity were focused on in this sermon?

   _____
   _____
   _____

Dr. J. A. Gladney

_____
_____

4. Did this sermon move you to take action to unify an area in our community? Explain.

_____
_____
_____
_____
_____

Pre-Test Questions

Name_____   Date_____

This form is intended to inform and assist in gathering needed information. Your honesty is appreciated. Please rate the following items according to scale: 1= not true 10=true

1. I know what multilateral ecumenical unity is.

    1 2 3 4 5 6 7 8 9 10

2. I know what oikoumene is.

    1 2 3 4 5 6 7 8 9 10

3. Churches uniting in dialogue with each other the common goal of ministry indicates.

    A. A loss of hope within the individual churches.

    1 2 3 4 5 6 7 8 9 10

    B. A desire to enrich the other church or churches and further the kingdom of God.

    1 2 3 4 5 6 7 8 9 10

    C. A sign of weakness or desperation in a declining church.

    1 2 3 4 5 6 7 8 9 10

4. Churches which unite for a common cause for a greater good

A. Inspire each other to establish new goals and objectives.

1 2 3 4 5 6 7 8 9 10

B. Have trouble agreeing on mutually satisfying goals and objectives.

1 2 3 4 5 6 7 8 9 10

C. Both of the above.

1 2 3 4 5 6 7 8 9 10

D. Neither of the above.

1 2 3 4 5 6 7 8 9 10

5. If my church works with other groups in the community to cause change(s), I will.

A. Be very happy.

1 2 3 4 5 6 7 8 9 10

B. Be very unhappy.

C. Other_____

6. How do you feel about the lack of unity among the churches and Pastors in Griffin and Spalding County?

A. Be very pleased.

1 2 3 4 5 6 7 8 9 10

B. Be very displeased.

1 2 3 4 5 6 7 8 9 10

7. How would you feel about participating in a joint or cooperative ministry effort?

   A. Very Eager

   1 2 3 4 5 6 7 8 9 10

   B. Eager

   1 2 3 4 5 6 7 8 9 10

   C. Indifferent

   1 2 3 4 5 6 7 8 9 10

   D. Apprehensive

   1 2 3 4 5 6 7 8 9 10

8. What do you see yourself doing to help in the process of unifying our community?

   _____
   _____
   _____
   _____
   _____
   _____

9. Churches should become more visible in our communities.

   1 2 3 4 5 6 7 8 9 10

10. Visibility will help in a unifying effort.

1   2   3   4   5   6   7   8   9   10

11. Your Age: 20-30, 31-40, 41-50, 51-60, 61-70, 71-80, 80+

Pre-Test Analysis

Name_____   Date_____

This form is intended to inform and assist in gathering needed information. Your honesty is appreciated. Please rate the following items according to scale: 1=not true 10=true

1. I know what multilateral ecumenical unity is.

1 2 3 4 5 6 7 8 9 10

2. I know what oikumene is.

1 2 3 4 5 6 7 8 9 10

3. Churches uniting in dialogue with each other for the common goal of ministry indicates.

   A. A loss of hope within the individual churches.

   1 2 3 4 5 6 7 8 9 10

   3-Not sure

   B. A desire to enrich the other church or churches and further the kingdom of God.

   1 2 3 4 5 6 7 8 9 10

   C. A sign of weakness or desperation in a declining church.

   1 2 3 4 5 6 7 8 9 10

   2-Not sure

4. Churches with unite for a common cause for a greater

good.

A. Inspire each other to establish new goals and objectives.

1 2 3 4 5 6 7 8 9 10

B. Have trouble agreeing on mutually satisfying goals and objectives.

1 2 3 4 5 6 7 8 9 10

2-No Answer

1-Not sure

C. Both of the above.

1 2 3 4 5 6 7 8 9 10

4-no answer

D. Neither of the above

1 2 3 4 5 6 7 8 9 10

4-No answer

5. If my church works with other groups in the community to cause change (s), I will.

   A. Be very happy.

   1 2 3 4 5 6 7 8 9 10

   B. Be very unhappy.

   1 2 3 4 5 6 7 8 9 10

4- no answer

C. Other_____

8- No answer

6. How do you feel about the lack of unity among the churches and Pastors in Griffin and Spalding County?

   A. Be very pleased.

   1   2   3   4   5   6   7   8   9   10

   3-no answer

   B. Be very displeased.

   1   2   3   4   5   6   7   8   9   10

   4-No answer

   C. Other_____

   D. 8-No answer

7. How would you feel about participating in a joint or cooperative ministry effort?

   A. Very eager

   1   2   3   4   5   6   7   8   9   10

   B. Eager

   1   2   3   4   5   6   7   8   9   10

   3- no answer

C. Indifferent

1　2　3　4　5　6　7　8　9　10

4- no answer

D. Apprehensive

1　2　3　4　5　6　7　8　9　10
4-no answer

8. What do you see yourself doing to help in the process of unifying our community?

_____
_____
_____
_____
_____
_____
_____
_____
_____
_____

9. Churches should become more visible in our communities.

1　2　3　4　5　6　7　8　9　10

10. Visibility will help in a unifying effort.

1　2　3　4　5　6　7　8　9　10

1- No answer

11. Your age: 20-30, 31-40, 41-50, 51-60, 61-70, 71-80, 81+

Pre-test

Scale of 1=10 1=not true 10=true

The results from the pre-test are as follows:

1. I know what multilateral ecumenical unity is. 7 scored 1, 1 scored 5 meaning they kind of knew what this term meant. However, the majority did not know what this term was or meant.

2. I know what oikumene is. 8 scored 1 meaning that they did not know what this term was at the beginning of this discussion.

3. Churches uniting in dialogue with each other for the common goal of ministry indicates:

   A. A loss of hope within the individual churches. 3 answered 1, 1 answered 6, 1 also answered 9, and 3 answered not sure meaning 3 of the surveyors does not see unity as a way of losing hope, while one of the surveyors answered 6 meaning they were leaning more toward the fact that unity was away of being a loss of hope, and 1 surveyors answered 9 meaning that surveyor felt it would be a loss of hope on the part of the church to unify with other churches. While three surveyors were not sure.

   B. A desire to enrich the other church or churches and further the kingdom of God. 1 answered 5, 8 answered 10, meaning one of the surveyors was kind of in the middle between sure and not sure about the desire of unity enriching the church or churches and unity being away to further the kingdom of God, while 8 surveyors were clear that unity with other churches would help further the kingdom of God.

C. A sign of weakness or desperation in a declining church 3 answered 1, 1 answered 2, 2 answered 10, 2 answered not sure meaning three surveyors was sure that unity is not a sign of weakness or desperation in a declining church while one person was almost sure because they answered 2 and 2 surveyors think that it is a sign of weakness and desperation in a declining church because they answered 10, while 2 of the surveyors were not sure they did not answer at all.

4. Churches which unite for a common cause for a greater good.

A. Inspire each other to establish new goals and objectives. 8 answered 10 meaning that unity will inspire the other churches to look critically at their objectives and cause much needed change within the church or churches.

B. Have trouble agreeing on mutually satisfying goals and objectives. 3 answered 1, 1 answered 5, 1 answered 8, 2 surveyors did not respond, 1 answered not sure meaning 3 of the surveyors do not think that the churches would have a problem agreeing on mutually satisfying goal and objectives, 1 of the surveyors was kind of in the middle while one of the surveyors thought that the group would find it difficult to agree on goals and objectives. While 2 did not answer and 1 was not sure.

C. Both of the above 1 answered 1, 1 answered 8, 2 answered 10, and there were 4 no answers, meaning they did not think either of the previous two question were true while three surveyors felt that both were somewhat agreeable, and 4 people did not put anything at all.

D. Neither of the above, 3 answered 1, 1 answered 9, and there were 4 no answers, meaning 3 surveyors felt neither of the above was true while 1 surveyor felt they both were true and 4 surveyors did not answer at all.

5. If my church works with other groups in the community to cause change (s), I will.

A. Be very happy, all of the surveyors said they would be very happy about working with other groups in the community to cause change.

B. Be very unhappy, 4 of the surveyors answered 1, and 4 had no answer meaning 4 of the surveyors said that they felt this question was not true, while four had no response at all.

C. Other, none of the surveyors wrote in a response for other.

Reconnecting the Local Church

6. How do you feel about the lack of unity among the churches and Pastors in Griffin and Spalding County?

   A. Be very pleased, 1 answered 1, 1 answered 7, 1 answered 8, 1 answered 9, and there were 3 no answers. This question had the greatest gap in responses, on person was ok with the lack of unity while 3 people had no comment at all and the others had mixed emotion.

   B. Be very displeased, 1 answered 1, 1 answered 5, 1 answered 7, 1 answered 10, and 4 no answer, meaning the answers for this question was spread out as well. Three of the eight was displeased while four of the eight had no response.

   C. Other, there were no write-in for this question at this time.

7. How would you feel about participating in a joint or cooperative ministry effort?

   A. Very eager 2 answered 1, 1 answered 8, 6 answered 10, this question showed that the majority of the surveyors would be very eager about participating in a joint or cooperative ministry effort.

   B. Eager, there was three no answers to this question, 3 answered 1, 1 answered 9, 1 answered 10, the majority of the surveyors were not sure about this question that is why they answered 1 for not true and the three no responses.

8. What do you see yourself doing to help in the process of unifying our community?

These are some samples of the response from question 8.

'Going into the community and being ready to help in any way we can as a church."

"I see myself visiting churches we normally do not fellowship with. I also see an opportunity to help in other ministries other churches are involved in."

9. Churches should become more visible in our communities, all 8 surveyors agreed that our churches should be more visible in our communities.

10. Visibility will help in a unifying effort. 7 of the eight surveyors agreed that visibility will help in a unifying effort.

11. Your Age: 1 of the surveyors are between the age of 20-30, 6 of the surveyors are between the age of 41-50, and 1 of the surveyors is 81 and above.

Post test analysis
Scale of 1-10 1=Not True 10=True

1. I know what multilateral ecumenical unity is. When the pre-test was done not many people had heard of multilateral ecumenical unity, and they did not know what it was. However, after the sermon series and Bible study that changed. One person chose 6, which says that they have a better understanding of what the term means, while 6 of the persons doing the survey chose 10 meaning they now know what the term now means and have a better knowledge of a working definition of the term.

2. I know what oikumene is. When the pre-test was given none of the surveyors had any understanding of the term oikumene. It was a new term to them, and they seemed excited to learn about new concepts concerning unity. At the end of the sessions one person still was unclear about the term they chose 3 while the other participants chose 10 meaning that they now have a greater understanding of oikumene.

3. Churches uniting in dialogue with each other for the common goal of ministry indicates:

    A. A loss of hope within the individual churches. This question in the pre-test had a variety of responses. The writer does not know if it was because the surveyors did not understand the question or what the case was. The response from the post-test had a wide range of answers as well. 3 of the surveyors answered 1 meaning that they did fell it would be a lost of hope within the individual churches. While on the other hand on of the surveyors answered 9 and 3 did not response to the question at all. This could mean that they feel that churches should not unit or that they would experience a loss of hope within the individual congregations.

B. A desire to enrich the other church or churches and further the kingdom of God. 1 of the surveyors answered 9 and 6 answered 10, meaning that unity will create a desire to enrich other churches and further the kingdom of God.

C. A sign of weakness or desperation in a declining church. This question had a wide range of responses from those answering the questions. 3 of the surveyors answered 1 meaning they felt it was not or would not be a sign of weakness or desperation on the part of a declining church. However, there were 3 surveyors that did not answer this question and 1 that answered 10. The person that answered 10 fills that it is a sign of weakness or desperation on the part of a declining church. However, the majority of the surveyors felt it was not.

4. Churches which unite for a common cause for a greater good:

A. Inspire each other to establish new goals and objectives. All of the surveyors were clear on this question. They all answered 10. Which says that unity will inspire other churches to establish new goals and objectives and cause the churches to come out of their individual boxes.

B. Have trouble agreeing on mutually satisfying goals and objectives. 2 of the surveyors answered 1 and 1 of the surveyors answered 3, meaning they didn't fill that if churches united, they would have trouble agreeing on mutually satisfying goals and objectives. While 1 of the surveyors answered 10 and three did not respond. That is half of the surveyors for that question that is unsure even after going through the bible study and listen to the sermon series.

C. Both of the above, this question had a wide range of responses even after the session was over. 1 of the surveyors answered 1, 1 answered 5, 1 answered 19, and four did not respond. That is odd because in the pretest four people did not respond either. The conclusion that the writer drew from this was that those people taking the survey did not understand this question or it could mean that their mind set did not change concerning this question.

D. Neither of the above, 2 of the surveyors answered 1, 1 answered 4, and four did respond at all.

5. If my church works with other groups in the community to cause change (s), I will

A. Be very happy, all of the surveyors answered 7 meaning they would be ok with the idea of their church working other groups in the community to cause change(s).

B. Be very unhappy, 3 of the surveyors answered 1, and 4 of the surveyors did not respond.

C. Other, there were 6 no answers to this question and 1 surveyor said they was excited because we can spread the good news.

6. How do you feel about the lack of unity among the churches and Pastors in Griffin and Spalding County?

A. Be very pleased, 1 answered 1, 1 answered 2, 2 answered 10, and 2 did not respond. Meaning that the majority of the surveyors are not pleased with the lack of unity among pastors and churches in the Griffin area.

B. Be very displeased, the question had the same as the above question in response. The majority of the surveyors answered either 9 or 10, meaning they are very displeased about the lack of unity in this area.

C. Other, there were 6 no answered to this question and 1 response was we need more togetherness.

7. How would you feel about participating in a joint or cooperative ministry effort?

Very eager, 2 of the surveyors answered 9, and 4 answered 10, meaning that they would be ok with participating in a joint or cooperative ministry effort.

However, 1 of the surveyors did not answer at all.

Eager, the majority of those that took the survey was or would be eager about the before mentioned question. The surveyor's response were 1 answered 8, 1 answered 9, 2 answered 10, and 3 did not response.

Indifferent, 2 answered 1, and 1 answered 3, and 4 did not response.

Apprehensive, 2 answered 1, 1 answered 6, and 4 did not response.

8. What do you see yourself doing to help in the process of unifying our community?

   These are some of the responses from this question: "I plan to work with my leaders and do whatever they feel I can do to help my community and church. I will invite more people to visit my church as well as support their own ministry. I plan a become more involved in community affairs." "I plan to help us become a stronger voice by getting the word out to others about what is going on in the community?" "Encourage each other and talking with them."

9. Churches should become more visible in our communities, all the surveyors agreed that the churches should become more visible in the community.

10. Visibility will help in a unifying effort. This question also drew the same response from all the persons taking the survey. They all agreed that the visibility of

the churches will help in a unified effort to bring about change in our communities.

11. Your age: 1 of the surveyors are between the age of 20-30, 5 of the surveyors are between the age of 41-50, and 1 of the surveyors is 81 above.

Bibliography

Alan Richardson, J. B. (1983). *the Westminster Dictionary of christian Theology.* Philadelphia: The Westminster Press.

Alan Richardson, J. B. (1983). *The Westminster Dictionary of Christian Theology.* Philadelphia: The Westminster Press.

Bria Ion, H. D. (1995). *Ecumenical Pilgrims Profiles of Pioneers in Christian Reconciliation.* Geneva: WCC Publication Geneva.

Brown, R. (1967). *The Ecumenical Revolution: An Interpretation of the Catholic Protestant Dialogue.* New York: Doubleday and Company.

Cardinal Augustine Bea, H. W. (1967). *Peace Among Christians.* New York: Herder and Herder Association Press.

Carlo, F. (1664). *Pope John and the Ecumenical Council.* New York: The World Publicizing Company.

Cougar, Y. (1964). *Dialogue Between Christians.* Westminster: 1964.

Ellingsen, M. (1999). *Reclaiming Our Roots an Inclusive Introduction to Church History.* Harrisburg: Trinity Press Intenational.

Erica C. Lincoln, L. H. (1990). *The Black Church in the African American Experience.* Raleigh: Duke University Press.

Faulkner, R. D. (1990). *Griffin's 150 Years of Seasoning.* Georgia: Faulkner Publishing.

Ford, D. F. (1997). *The Modern Theologians.* Malden: Blackwell Publishers.

Freedman, D. N. (1992). *The Anchor Bible Dictionary Volume 6 Si-Z.* New York: Doubleday Publishing Group Inc.

Freedman, D. N. (1992). *The Anchor Bible Dictionary Volume 6 Si-Z.* New York: Double Day Publishing Group Inc.

Gerald, P. (1992). *In One Volume the NIV Matthew Henry Commentary.* Grand Rapids: Zondervan Publishing House.

Gibson, A. F. (1992). *When Christians Disagree the Church and Its Unity.* England: InterFaith Press.

Gonzalez, J. L. (1985). *The Story of Chistianity Volumbe 2 The Reformation to the Present Day.* New York: Harper San Francisco Publishers.

Goodwin, E. (1995). *The New Hiscox Guide for Baptist Churches.* Valley Forge: Johnson Press.

Hunt, G. L. (1963). *A Guide to Christian Unity.* St. Louis: Bethany Press.

Jackson, C. (1996). *Straight Talk on Touch Topics.* Grand Rapids: Zondervan Publishing House.

Jurjii, E. (1982). *The Ecumenical Era in Church and Society.*

New York: MacMillan Company.

Kinnamon, M. (1982). *Towards Visible Unity Commission on Faith and Order.* Lima: World Council of Churches.

Lambert, B. (1967). *Ecumenism Theology and History.* New York: Herder and Herder.

Mark, E. (1999). *Reclaiming Our Roots and Inclusive Introduction to Church History, from Martin Luther to Martin Luther King Jr.* Harrisburg: Trinity Press International.

McAfee, B. R. (1969). *Ecumenical Revolution an Interpretation of the Catholic.* London: Burns & Oates.

McNeal, R. (2009). *Present Future Six Tough Questions for the Church.* Jossey-Bass.

Meyer, H. (1999). *That All May Be One Perceptions and Models of Ecumenicity.* Grand Rapids: William B. Eerdmans Publishing Company.

Modras, R. (1968). *Paths to Unity American Religion Today and Tomorrow.* New York: Sheet and Ward.

Ola Tjorhom, G. W. (2004). *Visible Church-Visible Unity: Ecumenical Ecclesiology and "the Great Tradition of the Church".* Collegeville: Liturgical Press.

Others, B. J. (1968-2000). *A History of the Ecumenical Movement Volume 3.* Geneva: WCC Publications Geneva.

Peter C. Hodgson, R. H. (1982). *Christian Theology: An*

Introduction to Its Traditions and Task. Minneapolis: Fortress Press.

Redford, D. (2005-2006). *Standard Lesson Commentary.* Cincinnati: Standard Publishing Company.

Shelley, B. L. (1982). *Updated 2nd Edition Church History in Plain Language.* Dallas: Word Publishing.

Smiley, T. (2002). *Keeping the Faith.* New York: Random House.

William, E. (1966). *Baptist and Christian Unity.* Nashville: Boardman Press.